MOST[illegible]
DOWNHILL

~

leisurely walks in the Lake District

Alan Pears

Published by Sigma Leisure – an imprint of
Sigma Press, 1 South Oak Lane, Wilmslow, Cheshire SK9 6AR, England.

British Library Cataloguing in Publication Data
A CIP record for this book is available from the British Library.

Reprinted with minor corrections 1995

ISBN: 1-85058-371-4

Typesetting and Design by: Sigma Press, Wilmslow, Cheshire.

Maps and photographs by: Alan Pears

Cover by: Martin Mills

Printed by: Manchester Free Press

General Disclaimer

Whilst every effort has been made to ensure that the information given in this book is correct, neither the publisher nor the author accept any responsibility for any inaccuracy.

Preface

Walking 'Mostly Downhill' in the Lake District? There are, thank goodness, no chair lifts here, so how is it possible to achieve this most pleasant experience?

A car and a companion are all you need. Except for one, each walk described here has a setting-down point which is at a higher altitude than the picking-up point. Though distances are short, the beauty of the landscape and the views from the paths offer to walkers a true experience of the district and a real sensation of having been in the fells.

The classic, big walks are well-enough known and copiously described. There is more to the Lake District, though, and even visitors with tough and magnificent walking in mind should not leave without some acquaintance with the meadows, the tiny bridges over small streams, the old stone stiles deftly cut into walls, churches in stunning settings and the quiet woods. These walks encompass such places.

Vigorous and fit walkers, without encumbrances, might choose a 'Downhill' for a post-prandial summer stroll or for a safer walk on a drenching day. There are others, limited by age, lessening fitness or the company of young children for whom the walks could be their expedition for the day.

And what about first-timers and day-trippers? It's a pity so many wander round the shops or just ask 'the way to the lake' when, with a guide and the smallest of effort they could be off-road. Groups of younger children, if they are not to be deterred for life, need a gentle start on the fells. Older residents, sharing the glory of the district with their visiting friends and relations, require routes which are not too demanding, paths which offer high dividends for effort invested.

On a good day, and in the right circumstances, walkers may wish to go down and up again, or up and down again. Drivers may do parts at the beginning or the end. The walks are indications of what is possible.

My research began with the onset of angina. I had the need and the desperate desire to walk. The uphill toll was too great. So it was especially with afflicted people in mind that I compiled this book. It was in the walking of it that I met the fit, the aged, the papoosed babies, the blind and the Special School children, all revelling in the freedom of the fells.

These walks could not have been planned, walked or recorded without great help from my wife. I am indebted to the rest of my family for their encouragement.

Alan Pears

CONTENTS

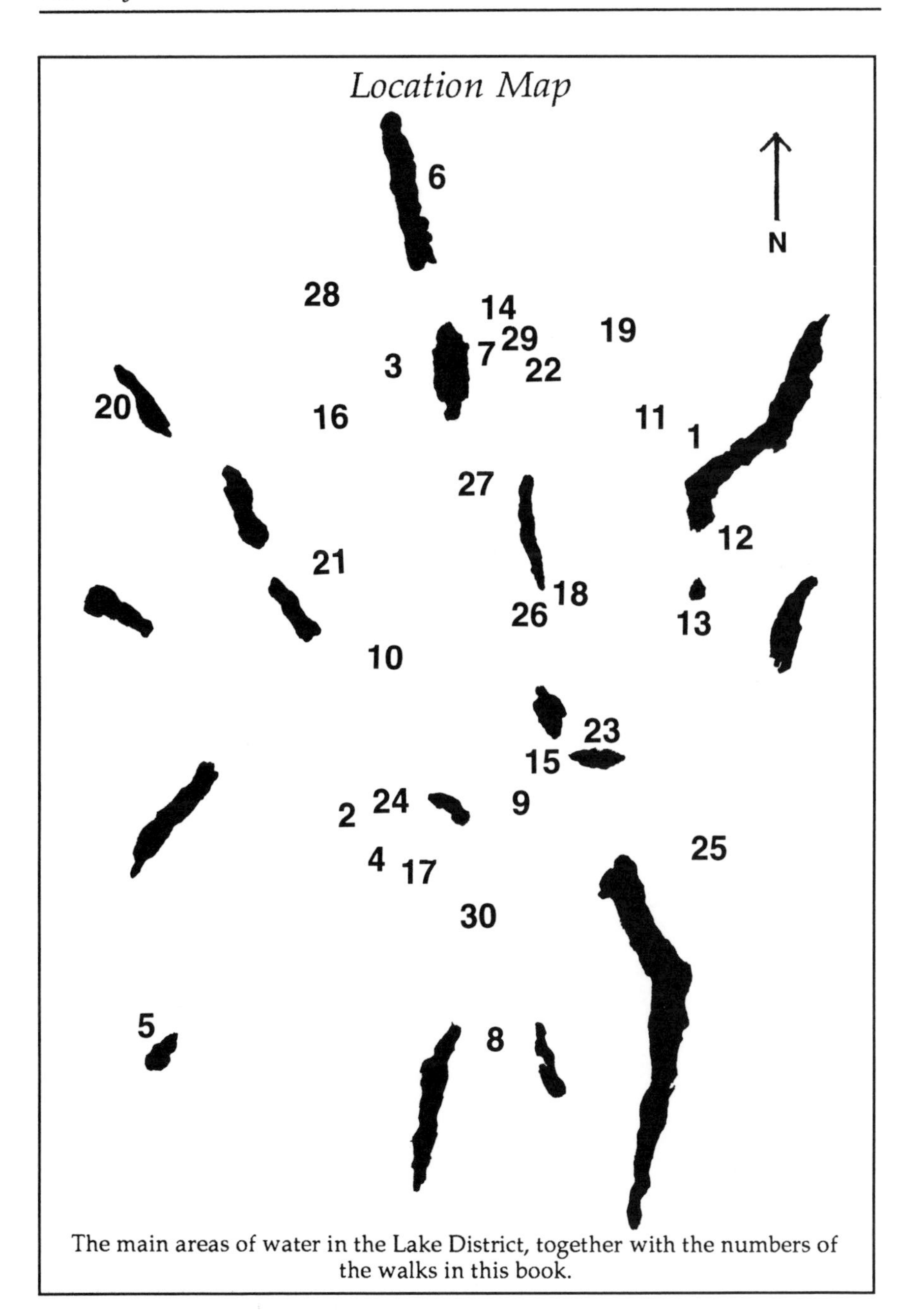

The main areas of water in the Lake District, together with the numbers of the walks in this book.

1. Dockray to Aira Force

Length of walk: 2 miles

Map ref: NY 393216 (Outdoor Leisure Map No 5)

Starting height: 950ft (289.5 m)

Finishing height: 500ft (152.4 m)

A welcome feature of this walk is the support available at the start and the finish. The Royal Hotel is at the beginning and a café and public toilets at the end. The terrain is mixed – worn path over open fields, woodland paths where care must be taken if exposed roots look slippery, and rocky outcrops demanding similar respect.

Two obvious stops are to view the rushing waters at High, and Aira Force. The closeness of Gowbarrow on the left and the Hows on the right make for a sheltered walk – but not, of course, from the district's armoury of rain!

Driver

Dockray is situated on the A5091. It can be reached from the A66 by turning at a point midway between Keswick and Penrith, or by travelling $1^1/_2$ miles up from the A592 lakeside road.

The dropping-off point is to the south and just over the bridge in the centre of the village. There is parking space for about six cars on the east side of the road.

The picking-up point can be reached by merely going down the A5091 until the lakeside A592 is reached. Turning left, about 40 yards on, you will find a large car park. There is a café (open at holiday times) and toilets.

The Walk

1. The walk starts from the centre of Dockray. A lane opposite the Royal Hotel is signposted 'Aira Force', and it is between houses that the lane leads to Aira Beck.

2. When the last house is passed the path bears to the right and slightly uphill.

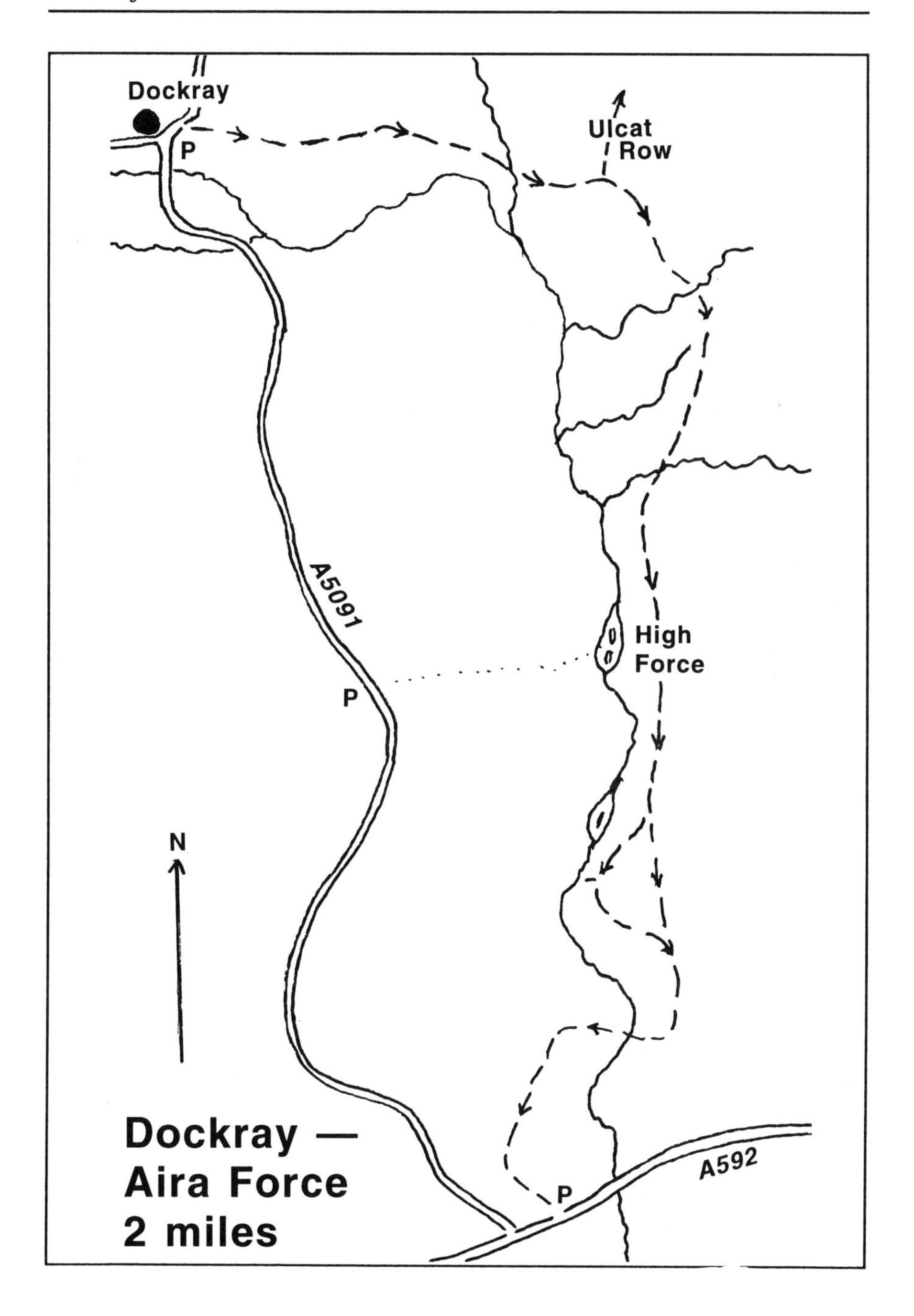
Dockray
P
Ulcat
Row
A5091
High
Force
P
N
A592
P
Dockray —
Aira Force
2 miles

3. The way is through a gate and on to open land. As the trees are reached a further gate lets you on to National Trust land. Take plenty of time to look at the views ahead and to identifying the fells on the sky line.

4. There is a constant sound of water to your right. It is worth examining the deep gullies caused by water movement through the ages. Most particularly, it is interesting to see the different coloured rock in the river bed at High Force. You begin to see more of the lake as you proceed down the path.

Aira Force

5. Watch for a wicket gate across a green sward. It is through this that Aira Force can be visited with its falls and picturesque bridge.

6. Regain the main path and go through another wicket gate. From here it is an interesting walk down steps and across a bridge to the car park.

2. Blea Tarn

Length of walk: $1^1/_2$ miles

Map ref: NY 291051 (Outdoor Leisure Map No 6)

Starting height: 735ft (224 m)

Finishing height: 550ft (167.6m)

The walk is on the bridge of hummocky land connecting the Great and Little Langdale Valleys. The tarn lies in a slight hollow at the upper end of an indent scooped out when moving ice was shaping both valleys. On a good day, the tarn shore is a perfect resting place, and the immediate area with its backcloth of Pikes, a classic for photographers.

'Beneath our feet a little lowly vale . . .
A liquid pool that glittered in the sun
And one bare dwelling. One abode, no more'.

from 'Excursion', William Wordsworth

Leaving the tarn, the gurgling waters of the often deep-set Blea Moss Beck provide a cheerful accompaniment.

Good footwear is important. Do not let short distances lull you into disregard for comfort and safety.

Driver

The dropping point is at a cattle grid at the crown of the hill on the road from Great Langdale to Wrynose Pass.

To reach the picking-up point you need to go to the Wrynose Pass road then turn right. After passing Fell Foot Farm you carry on with a stone wall at the left side of the road. As you reach the end of the wall, beside a finger direction post, you will find parking space on either side of the road. This is the picking-up point.

The Walk

1. From the cattle grid, go down the side of the fence at right angles to the road.

2. The land round about is quite marshy but the path is well-defined and safe underfoot.

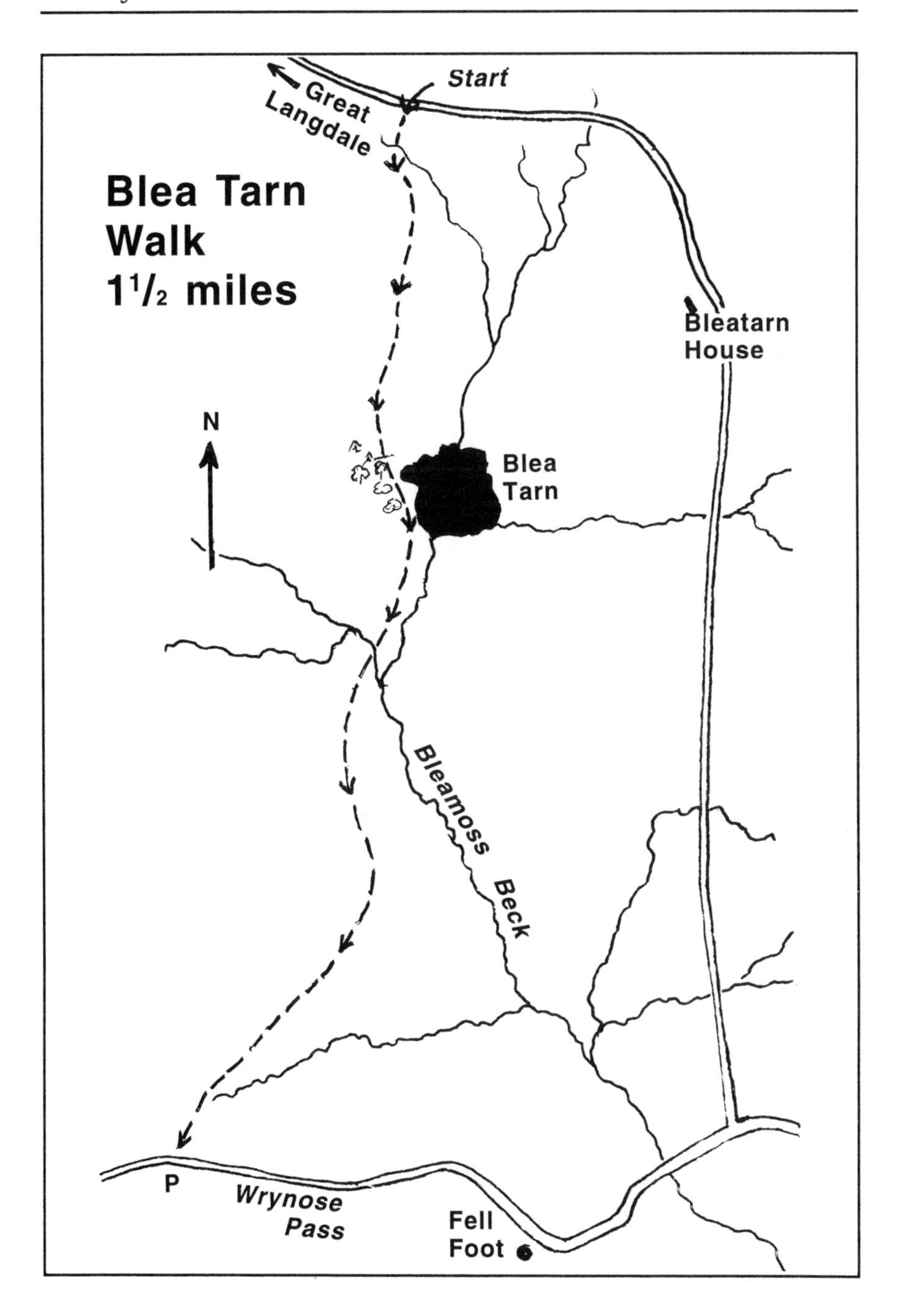
Start
Great Langdale
Blea Tarn Walk 1½ miles
N
Bleatarn House
Blea Tarn
Bleamoss Beck
P
Wrynose Pass
Fell Foot

3. Across the rough land and near the road you will see a farm house.

It was the cottage of Wordsworth's *Solitary* (The Excursion. Book 11, lines 638 – 684.)

4. As you approach the corner of the tarn you need to climb a stile. Ignore the path that goes uphill to the right.

5. Go down through a small wood of conifers. They soon give way to a plantation of rhododendron. These were planted by the Victorians who disliked the starkness of the fells.

6. A pleasant time can be spent, particularly by the young, in exploring by means of the many paths running through the plantation.

7. At the end of the plantation, turn left over a footbridge. Cross over a stile and you have access to the shores of the tarn.

8. The weather will really decide the time you spend here. Whether for a quick photograph, a stone skimming session or a picnic, this little divergence is well worth the time.

9. Return to the main path over the stile and footbridge and turn left.

10. For a time the path is quite tricky and all must concentrate where feet are placed. It is however a sheltered part of the walk and there is much to see and study nearby.

11. As the beck turns away from the path so the view opens up. Underfoot it is perhaps a little damper but shelter from the west is maintained by the fell side.

12. The path becomes less distinct as the boggy land has resisted the efforts of countless walkers to make their mark.

13. As you approach the Wrynose Road, and your pick up point, keep to the thinly marked path to avoid the marshy land on either side.

3. Catbells to Little Town

Length of walk: $1^1/_2$ miles

Map ref: NY 247212 (Outdoor Leisure Map No 4)

Starting height: 500ft (152.4 m)

Finishing height: 390ft (118.9 m)

There is an illusion of descent at the start of this walk. From the farm road you look down into Newlands and see, here and there, the roofs of houses and farms and a large stretch of the valley floor. Ahead lie the north west fells, with Causey Pike visible to the right, Knott Rigg, Robinson and Hindscarth in front and Dale Head just around the corner. On reaching Little Town the path is not much lower in altitude. Only after passing through the hamlet does the way drop more sharply to the end of the walk.

Driver

Leave the A66 to go down the west wide of Derwentwater through Portinscale. At a sharp uphill 'S' bend look for the right-hand turn off just after crossing a cattle grid. Take the turn off at the foot of Catbells. A sign informs you that parking is available 150 yards ahead. There is parking for about 10 cars. This is your dropping point.

Go back along the narrow road and turn back down the 'S' bend. After half a mile turn off left at a pointer to Stair. Pass the Swinside Inn and turn off left at a sign directing you to Little Town. This is a very winding narrow road. Go through Little Town to where the road descends on approaching a bridge over the Newlands Beck. There is a parking area for about 8 cars on the left – your picking-up point.

The Walk

1. Leave the car and continue along the road. It rises slightly. There are splendid views – to the right, Bassenthwaite Lake and the Newlands Valley; – looking back, first there is Swinside and Barff then Skiddaw and, well behind, Blencathra.

2. After about 500 yards the road ends at Skelgill. Here a grassy path goes off to the left and upwards. Ignore it and go through the gate towards the first house you see.

3. Go to the right of the house and you will see a finger post pointing along the side and to the back of it.

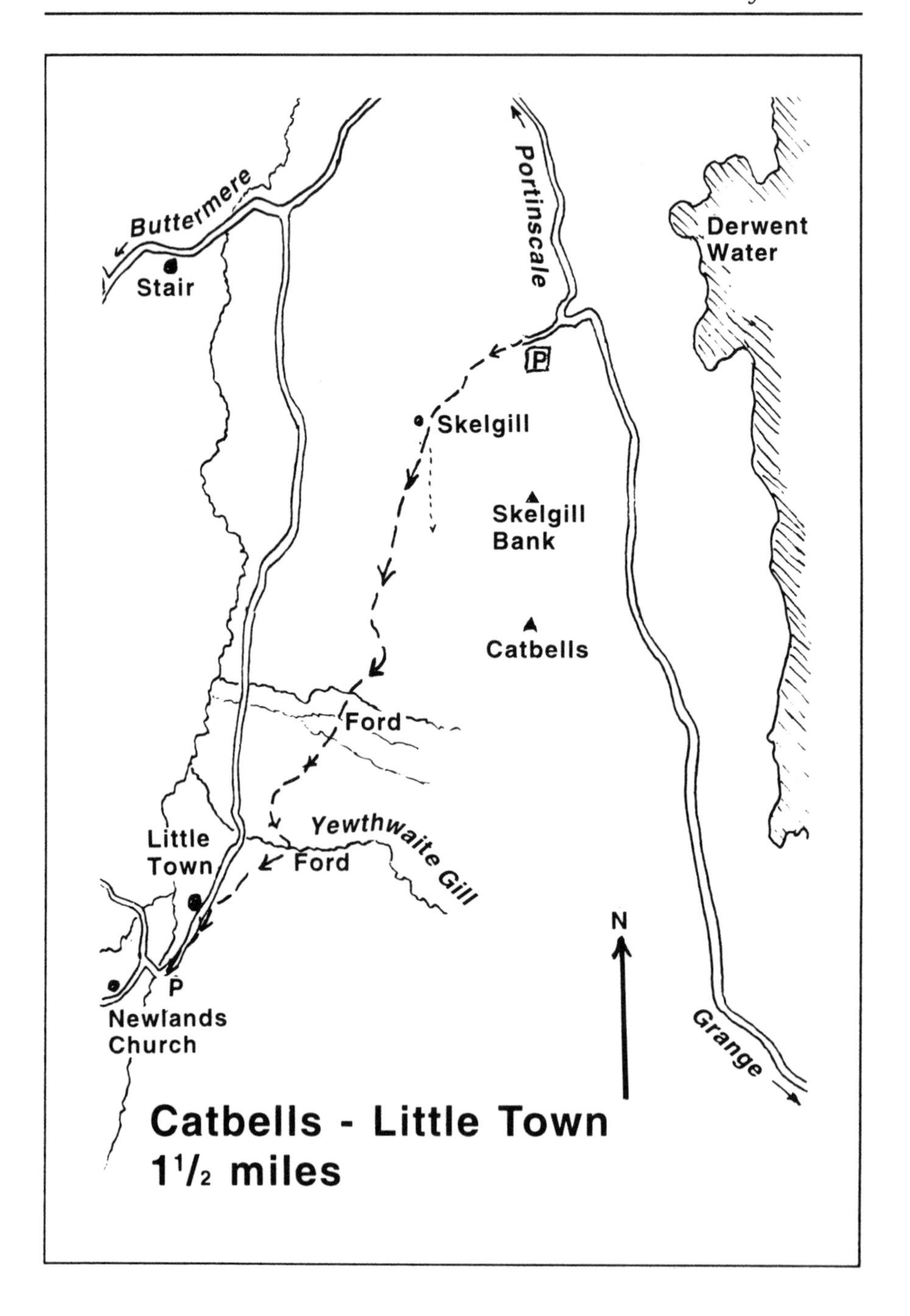
Buttermere
Stair
Portinscale
Derwent Water
P
Skelgill
Skelgill Bank
Catbells
Ford
Yewthwaite Gill
Little Town
Ford
P
Newlands Church
N
Grange
Catbells - Little Town
1½ miles

4. pass the family play area on your right and continue by a grassy path over a field to the first stile in the fence ahead of you.

5. The path goes straight ahead over three more stiles, then bears half-left to the next fence.

6. Follow the path along the side of an old Hawthorn hedge.

7. You can see the path ahead but pause awhile and look at the crescent of high fells ahead of you.

8. Go through the kissing gate and continue downwards on a grassy path until you reach a lane.

9. Pass the house and continue along the lane to a wooden bridge over Yewthwaite Gill.

10. Turn right and go down to the road. Turn left to Little Town and spend time wandering among the houses.

11. Continue along the road. You can see the car park on the left.

12. If you have time and have not, on a previous walk, seen Newlands Church, go ahead for 200 yards and turn left through a gate to view it and its surroundings.

4. Chapel Stile

Length of walk: $2^1/_2$ miles

Map ref: NY 322046 (Outdoor Leisure Map No 6)

Starting height: 400ft (121.9 m)

Finishing height: 260ft (79.2 m)

The woods here restrict the view of Lingmoor Fell, along whose lower slopes the walk lies – but keen bird spotters might see a jay!

There are glimpses, then full views of the high levels on the other side of the Langdale Valley. At the head of the walk is reached the Langdale Pikes and greater giants of the Central Fells come into view.

From afar, the village of Chapel Stile can be seen with its church perched above on the fell side. A pleasant picture is that of early morning haze around the house tops, together with the occasional curl of smoke produced by a burning wood fire.

Driver

Take the B5343 road along the Langdale Valley to Elterwater Village. Turn left and take the road signposted to Wrynose and Coniston. On leaving the village turn right on to a road marked 'Little Langdale'. After going 200 yards turn right again and start to climb on a narrow road. After nearly half a mile stop at a building on the right and where there is a road turning circle. This is the dropping point.

Go back to Elterwater and turn left on B5343 up the valley. At Chapel Stile there is parking in front of the Co-op shop. This is the picking-up point.

The Walk

1. Leave the car and go straight ahead. The walk starts very pleasantly through woods with the added advantage, on wet days, of a sound surface underfoot.

2. You leave the woods and walk to Baysbrown Farm between walls to where the road ends.

3. There is a slight rise in the path as you reach wooded land again.

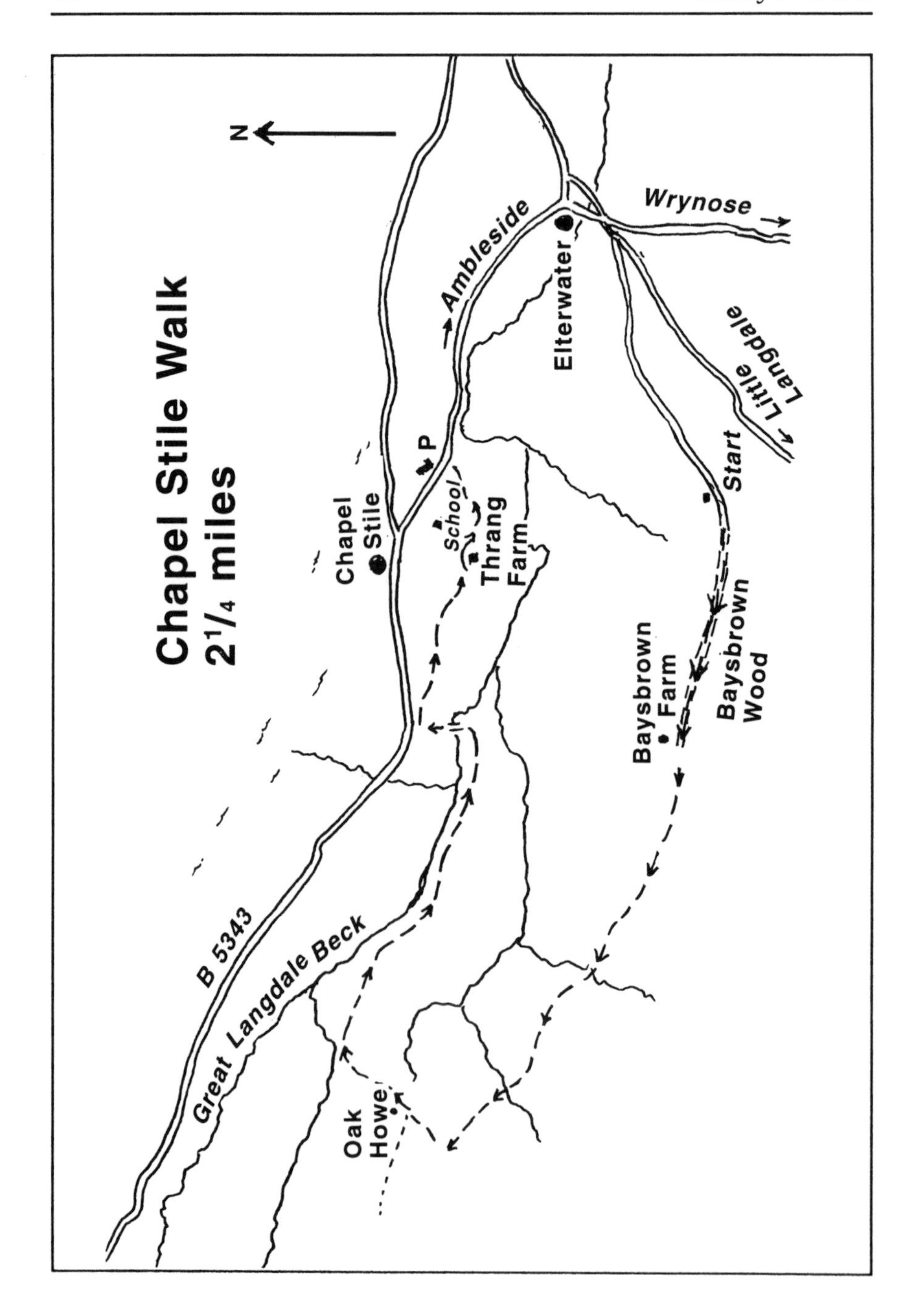

Chapel Stile Walk
2¼ miles
N
Ambleside
Wrynose
Elterwater
Little Langdale
Start
P
School
Chapel Stile
Thrang Farm
Baysbrown Wood
Baysbrown Farm
B 5343
Great Langdale Beck
Oak Howe

4. The woods give way at a stile to enclosed poor grass land. Continue along the stony path. It can be wet underfoot at certain times of the year.

5. Cross a stream then pass the old farm, Oak Howe. There is a broad path to your left; ignore this and continue ahead towards Great Langdale beck.

6. On a dry day this part of the walk is worth taking time over. Views towards the head of the valley are fine. The path takes you over open grass land back to the beck again.

7. Walk along the top of the retaining mound alongside the river. Turn left over a bridge then turn right.

8. The path then goes through a gate at the side of Thrang Farm, and continues to a metalled road. Go straight ahead.

9. Pass the burial ground on your right and continue over rough land alongside the school grounds.

10. At the main road, turn left towards the village. After a few yards you will see the Co-op shop on your right, your picking-up point.

5. Devoke Water

Length of walk: $4^1/_4$ miles

Map ref: SD 171977 (Outdoor Leisure Map No 6)

Starting height: 800ft (243.8 m)

Finishing height: 100ft (30.5 m)

The lake is set in the most desolate of moorland. Few trees are to be seen until you near the end of the walk. Man's hand is evident, both ancient and modern. Burial mounds and hut circles from Neolithic times are to be found there, and, to the west, the railway line crossing the Esk estuary can be seen.

Around the lake you must trust your map. Paths can be hard to discern. The wetness of the terrain has protected it from boot erosion. It also makes for comfortable, "soft" walking.

Driver

The walk starts on the Ulpha to Eskdale Road. The dropping-off point is at a small cross roads three miles from Ulpha. There is a parking area for about six cars on the corner of the road that runs to a farm.

To reach the picking-up point you must go straight on north west for two miles towards Eskdale. As you reach the valley floor, take a left turn on an even narrower road. This runs along the side of the River Esk for three miles until the main A595 is reached. Turn south for three quarters of a mile when the entrance to Dyke Farm on the left is reached. There is ample parking space just off the road.

The Walk

1. The bridle path rises slightly for the first 200 yards then flattens out to an easy walk until the tarn comes into sight.

2. The path passes around the south side, and close to the edge, of the tarn – the ground being rather soft.

3. At the west end of the tarn there is a slight incline. The ground underfoot becomes rougher.

4. The path falls steadily. Time should be spent exploring Barnscar; in *'The Lake District'* by Millward & Robinson (Methuen), we learn that "the hut circles and walled enclosures at Barnscar point to a permanent settlement and here, archeologists have unearthed two Middle Bronze Age burial urns that help to date the occupation of the fells."

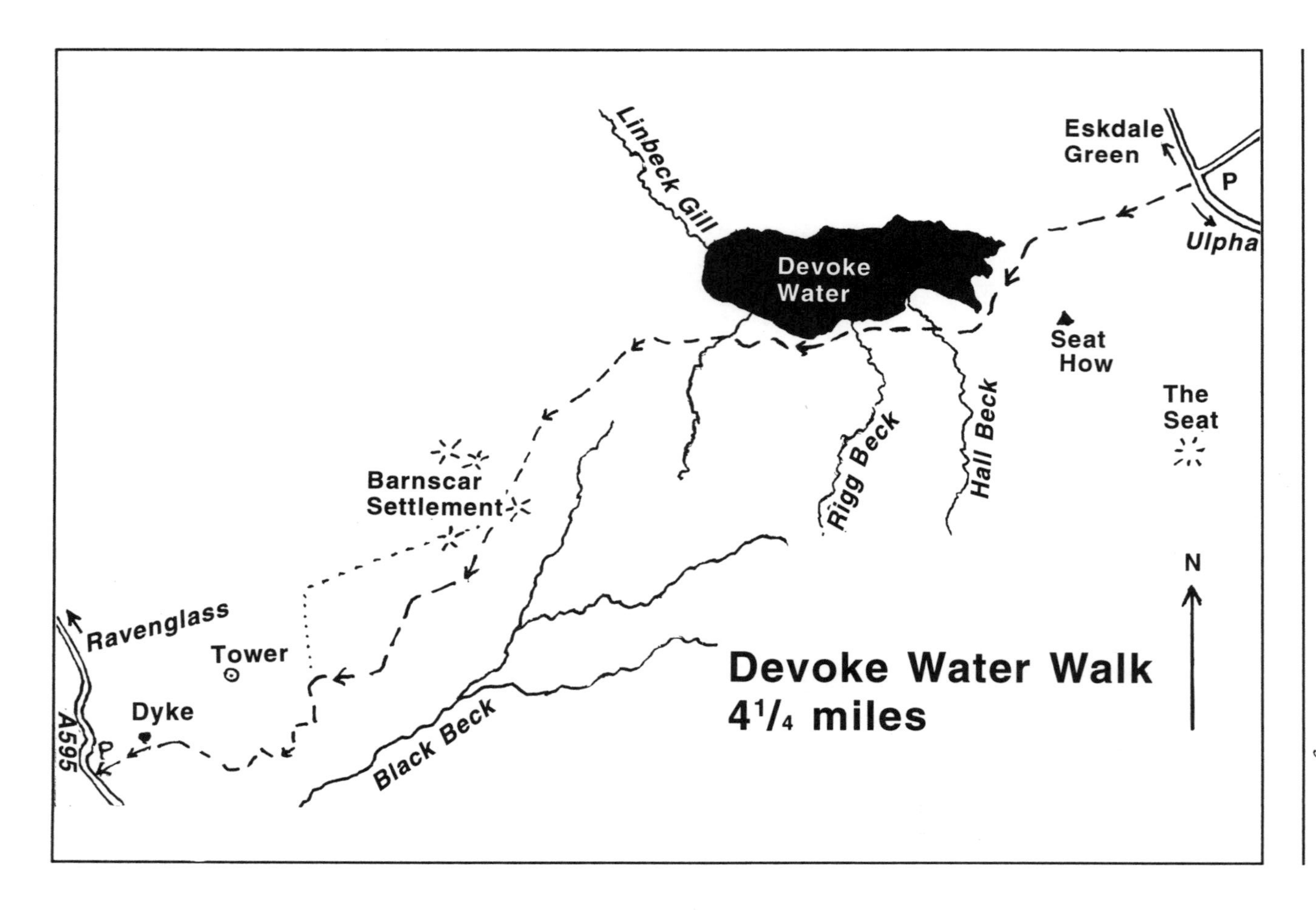
Eskdale Green
P
Ulpha
Linbeck Gill
Devoke Water
Seat How
The Seat
Rigg Beck
Hall Beck
Barnscar Settlement
N
Ravenglass
Tower
Dyke
A595
P
Black Beck
Devoke Water Walk
4 1/4 miles

5. The way on, is at first, steep then flat as a rather wet plain is reached. There are two paths across, both eventually leading to the same point. One goes due west until a well marked bridleway is reached, then you turn left. The other goes quite near, and follows the side of, a plantation. It eventually reaches the same bridlepath at a gate.

6. Through the gate the path runs between stone walls and from here on is well-defined.

7. There is a very good view straight ahead of the mouth of the Esk and the Eskmeal Viaduct. On the top of the fell to your right you will see an intriguing structure marked 'tower' on the O.S. map.

8. The path goes through the yard of Dyke Farm and on to the picking-up point on the A595.

6. Bassenthwaite Lake

Length of walk: $2^1/_2$ miles

Map ref: NY 235298 (Outdoor Leisure Map No 4)

Starting height: 360ft (109.7 m)

Lakeside level: 220ft (67.1 m)

Finishing height: 360ft (109.7 m)

The closeness of the western fringe of the National Park indicates that hills are giving way to coastal plain. The start and finish of this walk are at similar altitudes. The regaining of height is not to be feared.

Three points on the walk invite a pause: St Bega's church, with intriguing associations to be researched, the busy Calvert Trust (for the disabled), and Mirehouse. In season, refreshments are available at the Little Dodd Saw Mill at the side of the car park.

Driver

The A591 runs north from Keswick until it meets the A595 near Bothel. After travelling 4 miles northwards from Keswick, you will pass a narrow road to Scarness on your left. Continue along the main road for another half mile. As you approach an imposing Tudor style building (Ravenstone Hotel), you will see a small lay-by on your side of the road. This is the dropping point.

To reach the picking-up point you need to turn back towards Keswick. Just over a mile on, you will see signs on the left advertising Mire House and the Saw Mill café. Turn left into the Saw Mill grounds. There are two parking areas, a toilet block and, of course, the café. This is your picking-up point.

The Walk

1. From the layby walk forward along the road until you pass all of the buildings.

2. You will have passed a 'Permissive Path' sign – ignore it and continue until you see a finger post pointing down the side of the last building. Take this path.

3. The path continues diagonally through several small fields by way of wicket gates. Soon you will reach a narrow lane to Scarness. Cross over it to the path to St. Bega's Church.

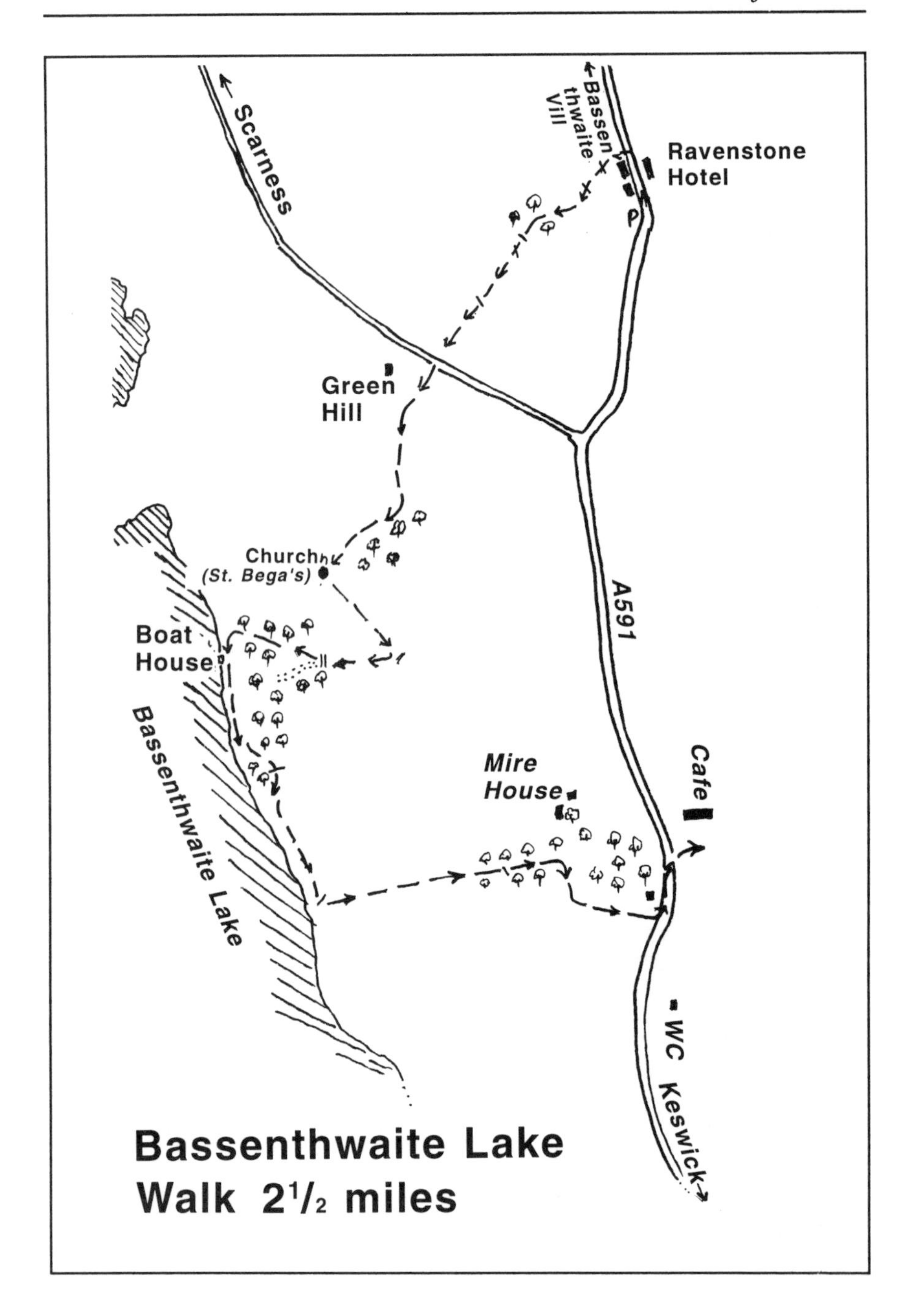
Scarness
Bassenthwaite Vill
Ravenstone Hotel
Green Hill
Church
(St. Bega's)
Boat House
Bassenthwaite Lake
A591
Mire House
Cafe
WC
Keswick
Bassenthwaite Lake
Walk 2½ miles

4. The ease of walking on this path gives you the chance to look around at the surrounding fells.

5. There is much of interest at the church and in its grounds. Take the broad flat path away from the church until you reach a path going to the right towards woods.

6. Go through the gate at the edge of the woods on to the broad path. After a few yards you will see a narrow path to the right.

7. This path will take you to the lakeside and to the boat house. A few yards further on you will see an interesting open-air amphitheatre in miniature.

8. Wend you way through the woods always keeping close to the lake until you reach a gate through which you walk on to grazing land.

9. Continue along the side of the lake. Here, there are splendid fells on either side of the lake with the nearest being the tree-covered Dodd.

10. Go through a fence and turn left as directed by a finger post. The way is slightly uphill. Enter the small wood by the wicket gate. Spring time sees the rhododendron at their best.

11. You will reach a drive. Turn right until you reach a fence. Turn left then and walk up the short grassy path to the gate. Go through the gate on to the main road.

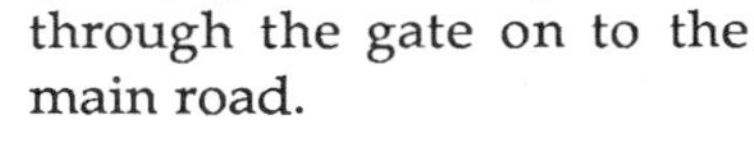

12. Your picking-up point is in the Saw Mill café area on the other side of the road. Take care when crossing the road, as traffic comes fast around the curve.

7. Great Wood

Length of walk: $1^3/_4$ miles

Map ref: NY 287227 (Outdoor Leisure Map No 4)

Starting height: 700 ft (213.3 m)

Finishing height: 350 ft (106.7 m)

The field path on the first part of the walk takes you from one valley going south, which includes Thirlmere, and the one crossed into Borrowdale, which includes Derwentwater. For almost the length of the walk the trees can be seen clinging to the side of Walla Crag (whose height is easily remembered – 1234ft). The path scores along the midriff of the fell. Views downwards are first to Bassenthwaite Lake and Keswick, and then to Derwentwater with its islands and its grandstand of the North West Fells.

Driver

The dropping point is on the A591 where Castle Lane meets the main road. There is room for two cars to pull off the road on the east side – but no space on the west side.

The picking-up point is in the Great Wood Car Park. Taking the A591 back towards Keswick and descending a steep hill, you can take the road marked – 'Town Centre via Manor Brow'.

As the first shops are reached, look out for the sign directing you to Borrowdale. Turn left there, then left again when you reach Fisher's shop. The road to Borrowdale is very picturesque but look for the sign on the left that says – 'Car Park 85 metres'. This is directing you to your pick up point.

The Walk

1. The walk starts where Castle Lane and the A591 meet. Leaving Keswick on the A591 road to Ambleside you have to travel almost 2 miles to reach the junction. There is a tiny lay-by accommodating two cars, but in crossing the road to start the walk, take care on this almost blind summit.

2. The sign post directs you towards Walla Crag, and the first 200 yards takes you ever so slightly uphill. The way is easy and the views are behind and to your left.

Near Castlerigg Farm

3. Following the grassy path you pass through, or over, four gates/stiles before reaching a minor road that leads to Rakefoot Farm.

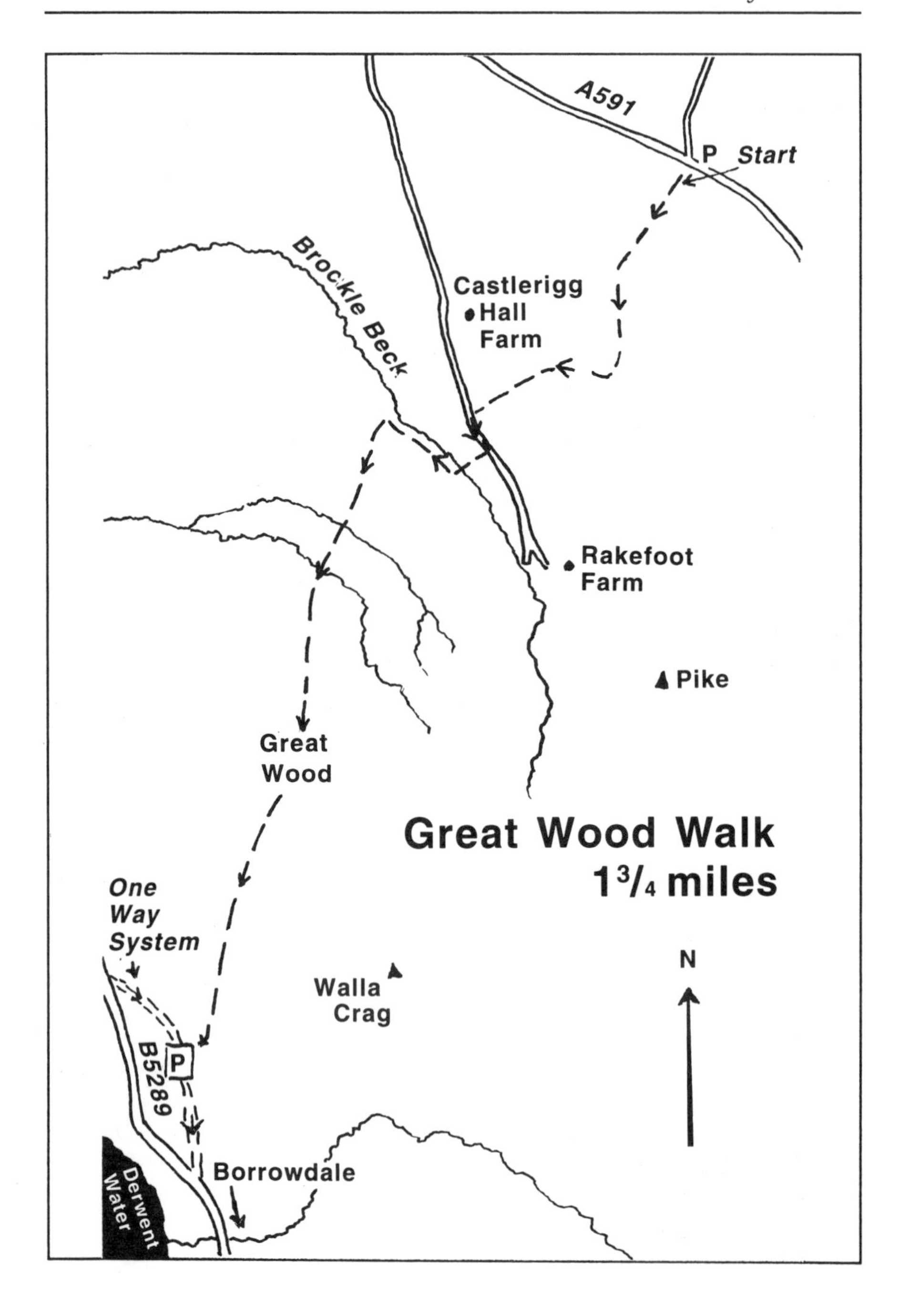
A591
P Start
Brockle Beck
Castlerigg
Hall
Farm
Rakefoot
Farm
Pike
Great
Wood
Great Wood Walk
1 3/4 miles
One
Way
System
Walla
Crag
N
P
B5289
Borrowdale
Derwent
Water

4. Turning left and taking only a few steps towards the farm, go through a stile to your right and on to a usually muddy patch leading to a wooden bridge astride Brockle Beck. Take the narrow path but keep to the right leg when the path appears to split at a rise 50 yards on from the bridge.

5. Follow a narrow path on the edge of the field. Views are to the west where you can see Derwentwater, the North-West Fells, and up to the Buttermere Fells through and beyond the Newland Valley.

Great Wood.

6. The path to Great Wood takes a left turn running alongside a wall. The entrance to the woods is over a rickety stile.

7. There is a gradual descent through the woods until the car park comes into sight. This is your picking-up point.

8. Grizedale to Hawkshead

Length of walk: 2 miles

Map ref: SD 343965 (Outdoor Leisure Map No 7)

Starting height: 660 ft (201.1 m)

Finishing height: 228 ft (69.5 m)

Grizedale Forest has something for everybody – from gift-shop browsers (check the opening times) to earnest orienteers. Paths for cyclists as well as walkers are well-signed, and once a year the forest is used in a stage of the Lombard Rally.

The last part of the walk has historic appeal, in the quaintness of Hawkshead's alleys and courts and in its association with the boyhood and education of William Wordsworth. He, as many boys were in their time at Hawkshead Grammar School, was boarded out with Ann Tyson.

In his Prelude he pays warm tribute to her. Returning there from his first year at Cambridge:

" . . . With eager footsteps I advance and reach
The cottage threshold where my journey closed.
Glad welcome had I, with some tears perhaps,
From my old Dame, so kind and motherly . . . "

"Childless, yet by the strangers to thy blood
Honoured with little less than filial love.
What joy was mine to see thee once again,
Thee and thy dwelling, and a crowd of things
About its narrow precincts all beloved . . . "

Driver

Going south leave Hawkshead by the road that goes down the west side of Esthwaitewater. After 500 yards, turn right at a sign directing you to Grizedale. The road is narrow and winding. Travel for one mile then turn right into the Moor Top Car park about 100 yards from the road. This is your dropping point.

If you are coming from the south then the car park is $2^1/_2$ miles from Satterthwaite and $1^1/_4$ miles from Grizedale Village.

To reach the picking-up point, turn back to Hawkshead and follow directions to the main car park.

The Walk

1. Walk on from the car park. Do not take the path going to the left.

2. There is a junction of 3 paths. Take the right-hand one and follow it as it slopes slightly uphill.

3. As you walk on, you have a wonderful view of the Pennines on the sky line to the right. Nearer to you, Esthwaitewater comes into view.

4. An 'S' bend in the path around the edge of a plantation gives you new views in the east.

5. The trees on your left have been recently felled. This makes for views of the Kirkstone Pass Inn, Windermere and Wansfell Pike.

6. A path joins from the left. Ambleside can be seen in the middle distance. Go on for 50 yards then turn off the forest road.

7. The path now becomes rougher and sometimes wetter. A seat has been thoughtfully placed on the side of the path for the weary.

8. The path crosses a stream, goes on to a wicket gate, then continues downhill with a wall to the right.

9. Forest trees are left behind and the path follows down the side of a stream. Hawkshead is now in sight.

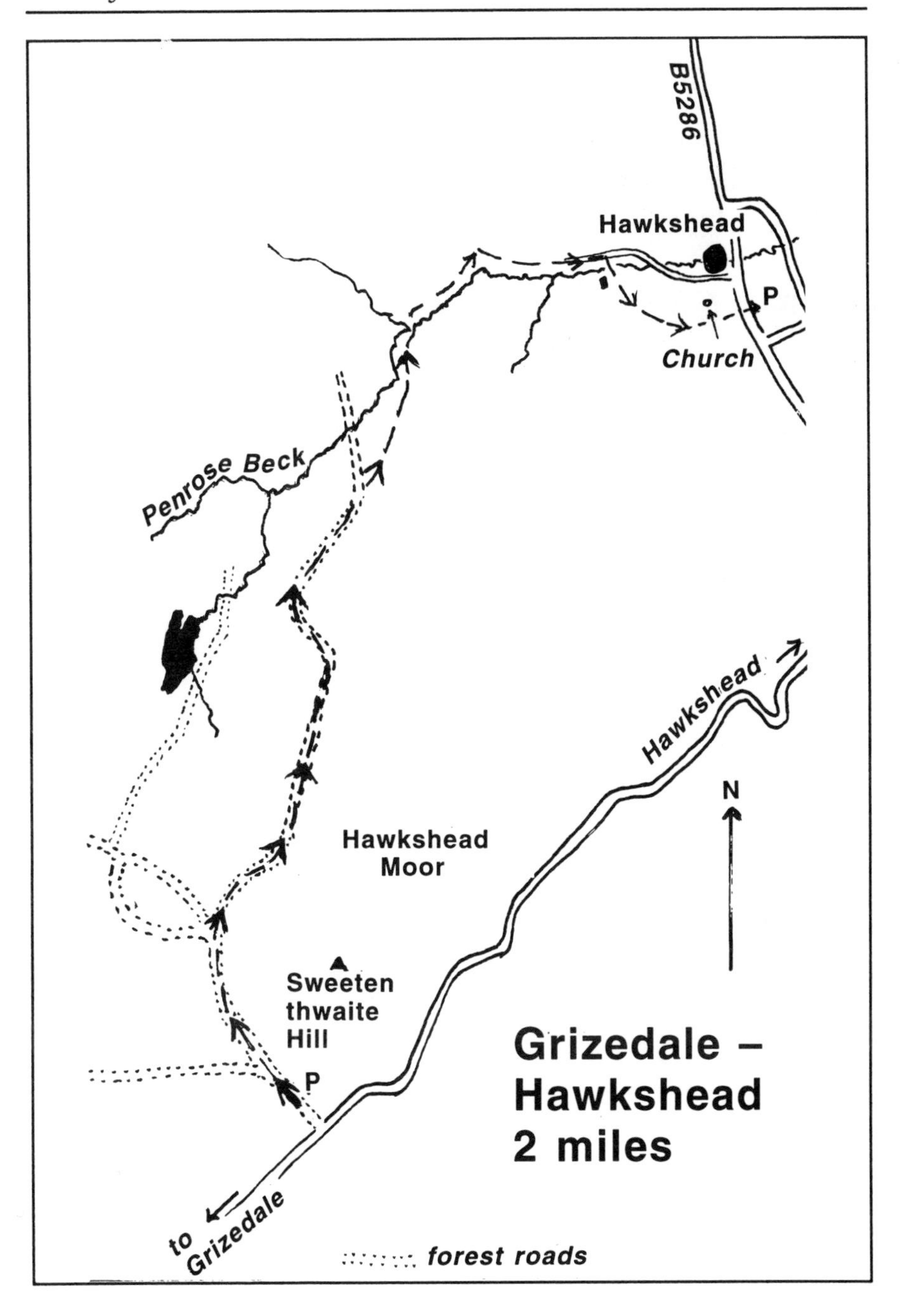
B5286
Hawkshead
P
Church
Penrose Beck
Hawkshead
N
Hawkshead
Moor
Sweeten
thwaite
Hill
P
Grizedale –
Hawkshead
2 miles
to
Grizedale
forest roads

Hawkshead Grammar School.

10. The path meets the road at the Old Vicarage. Turn right here then sharp left. The path leads you through two fields to the churchyard.

11. As you reach the church turn right down to the road. The car park – your picking-up point – is straight ahead.

9. High Close to Rydal

Length of walk: $2^1/_4$ miles

Map ref: NY 336053 (Outdoor Leisure Map No 7)

Starting height: 520 ft (158.5 m)

Finishing height: 165 ft (50.3 m)

The approaches from either Grasmere or Elterwater are winding with sharp bends, stretches of steep gradient, and walkers hugging the hedges to let you past. They are also short. Within a hundred yards of the start of the walk the scenery and distant views will more than compensate for the concentration of the drive. Much of Langdale is visible with Lingmoor Fell on its south side and Elterwater and the village. Water is a great feature of this outing: the path follows the western shore of Grasmere for a great part of it. The river between Grasmere and Rydal provides a final point of interest.

Driver

Take the road from Grasmere down the west side of the lake. Continue up Red Bank until you can take the right fork for Elterwater. You soon reach High Close Youth Hostel. About 150 yards further on you reach the highest part of the road. There is parking space where walkers can be dropped.

There are two ways of arriving at the picking-up point:

1. Turn round and go back to Grasmere Village. From here go on to the main A591 and head south. There are two sharp curves in the road around White Moss before you arrive at a car park on the right. There is a sharp turn in to it.

2. the other way is to go straight ahead to Elterwater. Turn left on the B5343, on to the A593 and so on to Ambleside. Turn north through Rydal Village. The lake is on your left and at its northern end there is a sharp left turn into the car park, your picking-up point. Unfortunately you now have to pay to park.

The Walk

1. Leave the car and, facing down the hill towards Elterwater Common, walk off in a half-right direction.

2. From the top of the first little knoll, there is a good view of the Langdale Pikes, and, to the left, of Lingmoor Fell.

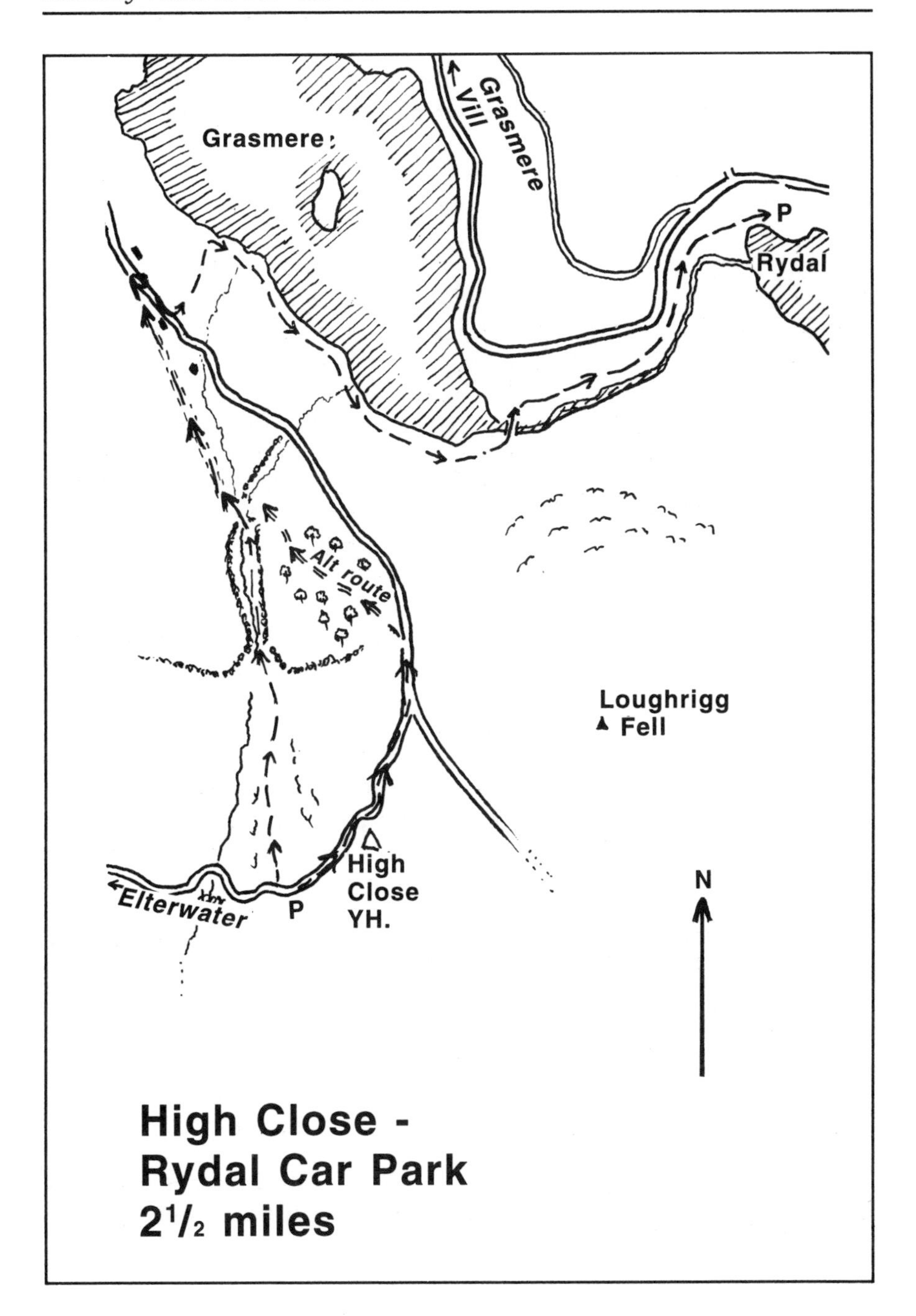
Grasmere
Grasmere Vill
P
Rydal
Alt route
Loughrigg Fell
High Close YH.
Elterwater
P
N
High Close - Rydal Car Park 2½ miles

3. The path goes on uphill slightly for about 100 yards. A path comes up from the left. Soon your path levels out and then turns downhill.

4. Paths running alongside a wall come in from both left and right. The area where they meet is rather wet, so take care. The walls end at a gate.

5. From the gate you can see Grasmere and beyond, Helm Crag and Dunmail Raise. Go through the gate into a narrow strip of land with path and beck running between walls.

6. At the end of the enclosure you merge with a path coming from Redbank Wood (see below). You now continue on a much wider lane.

7. Just as you reach the main road at Huntingstile Lodge, the path, itself, becomes a metalled road. Turn right on the road and look for a wall stile and gate 150 yards ahead. A sign directs you to the lake.

8. Go through and walk down to the shore of Grasmere. Turn right along the path.

9. You eventually reach the end of the lake. Go over the bridge and turn right, along the rugged path.

10. It is a pleasant and interesting walk to the car park, your picking-up point.

Alternative start

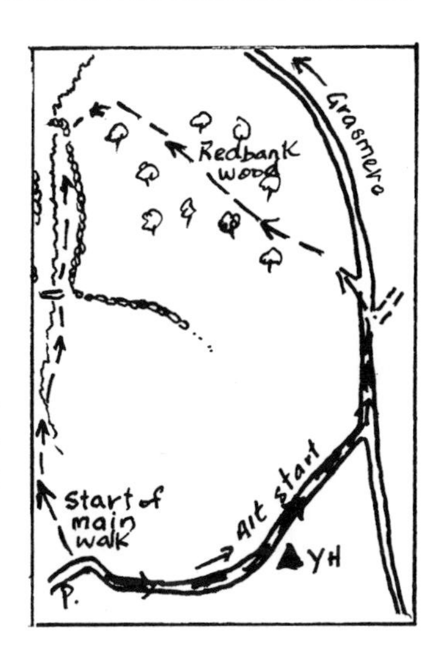

1. If you feel that the first 100 yards is too steep, then walk down the road, back past the youth hostel.

2. About 400 yards on from the hostel there is an opening on the left. A good path takes you down through Redbank Wood. Your path meets the main walk at the bottom of an enclosure just where a wide path begins.

10. Honister Hause to Grange

Length of walk: $3^1/_4$ miles

Map ref: NY 225135 (Outdoor Leisure Map No 4)

Starting height: 1190 ft (362.7 m)

Finishing height: 300 ft (91.5 m)

The car park here can be a windy spot. Don't be deterred. Try to take time before starting to observe the crags to the north west of the Hause. Slate was quarried from beneath the rear of Fleetwith Pike and there are signs all around of the industry. It is a world apart from the surroundings you are soon to gain. For anyone troubled, there are three "escape routes" on this walk.

First, after a mile and a quarter a short right-hand turn will take you to the hamlet of Seatoller. A mile further on there is a steep miners' track down to Rosthwaite. Thirdly, a metalled road from Grange back along the walk to Hollows Farm allows for a possible pick up.

For part of the walk you will be travelling on the Allerdale Ramble, a well-known longer distance walk, recorded on O.S. maps. You will be on the Ramble where the walk runs between the lower slopes of High Spy and Castle Crag. It is an eerie spot, but gives off satisfying echoes of the human or animal voice and clattering stones.

Driver

The dropping-off point is the car park behind the Youth Hostel situated at the top of Honister Pass on the B5289. To reach the Hause you can approach either from Buttermere Village in one direction or from Keswick, through the Borrowdale Valley, in the other.

Honister Youth Hostel

The picking-up point is reached by returning towards Keswick. Going only as far as Grange in Borrowdale, turn left over the bridge to the village. There is parking space immediately to the right at the end of the bridge. If the space is occupied there is more parking on the side of the lane to Hollows Farm reached by turning left just past the shop/café in the centre of the village.

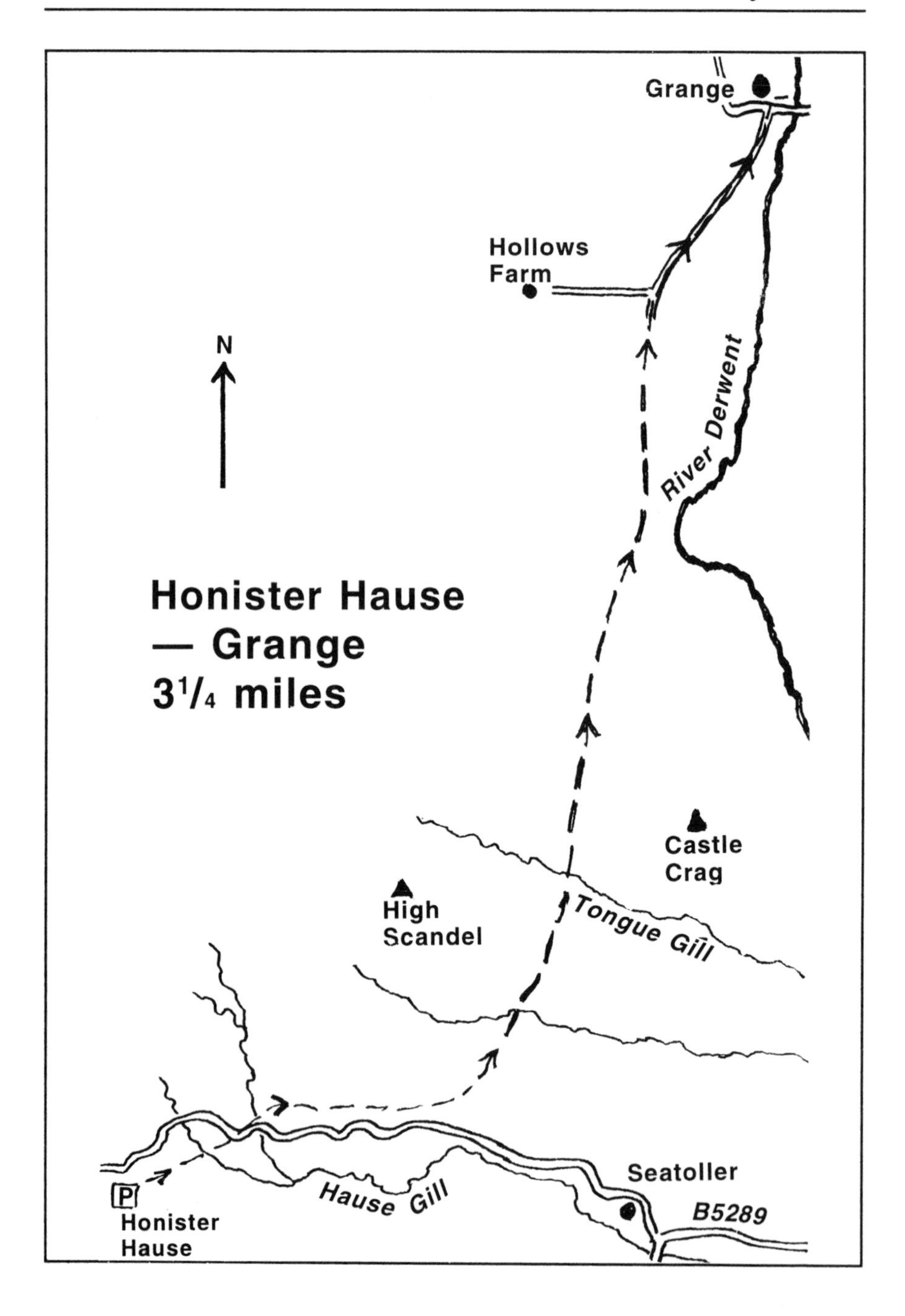
Grange
Hollows Farm
N
River Derwent
Honister Hause — Grange 3¼ miles
Castle Crag
High Scandel
Tongue Gill
Seatoller
P
Honister Hause
Hause Gill
B5289

The Walk

1. The walk starts at the car park. At its east end a path looking like an old waggonway begins, taking you towards Borrowdale.

2. The waggonway is easily identifiable running alongside and crossing the metal road.

3. After about three-quarters of a mile, the path finally turns away from the road.

4. At Tongue Gill you can, if need be, turn right to reach Rosthwaite (there is a public telephone and toilets). Otherwise, continue on what is part of the Allerdale Ramble.

Castle Crag

5. The path goes through a narrow pass with Castle Crag to the right. Forward, there is a narrow but interesting view right up to Skiddaw.

6. The path continues, keeping the mind agile, with its various surfaces underfoot, until the River Derwent is reached.

7. From here there is a pleasant, almost flat, walk to the village of Grange.

8. Ignore the left turn towards Hollows Farm, but continue on the metalled road. Near the village is a small car park on the left. Continue past until you reach the village street, where there are two sources of refreshment.

9. Your picking-up point may have been the car park you have just passed, or on a piece of land just to the left of the bridge.

11. Dowthwaitehead

Length of walk: $2^3/_4$ miles

Map ref: NY 380219 (Outdoor Leisure Map No 5)

Starting height: 1340 ft (408.5 m)

Finishing height: 1000 ft (304.8 m)

The crossroads from which the walk starts is also the end of the old coach road that runs from the Vale of St. John. Horsemire Head, the fell on the right, is a favourite place for not-too-serious skiing. In snowy weather a contraption is rigged up to get skiers to the top of their runs.

The hamlet of Dowthwaitehead, because of the fells surrounding it, is said to get no sun. There is water in plenty, with Rush Gill, Coegill Beck, Little Aira Beck and other, lesser streams all finding their way down past the hamlet to form Aira Force.

A quiet walk.

Driver

If approaching from the north, leave the A66 at Troutbeck and head south on the A5091. After two miles, turn off right at a signpost for Dowthwaitehead. Travel on for $1^1/_2$ miles until you reach a crossroads at High Row. This is the dropping-off point. If approaching from Ullswater travel north on the A5091 signposted for Dockray. When you reach the village, cross the bridge and immediately turn left at the Royal Hotel. Go up a narrow road until you reach High Row.

The picking-up point is reached by heading down the hill to Dockray. On reaching the Royal Hotel turn left. You are now on the A5091. Travel for half a mile to where the road splits. Go 50 yards up the left leg to a small lay-by on your left. This is your picking-up point.

The Walk

1. From the parking area, walk down the road signposted to Dowthwaitehead.

2. This is a walk, half of which is on metalled road, and the rest on field paths. The road is 'No Through' however, so very few vehicles use it.

3. Turn right at the first road junction

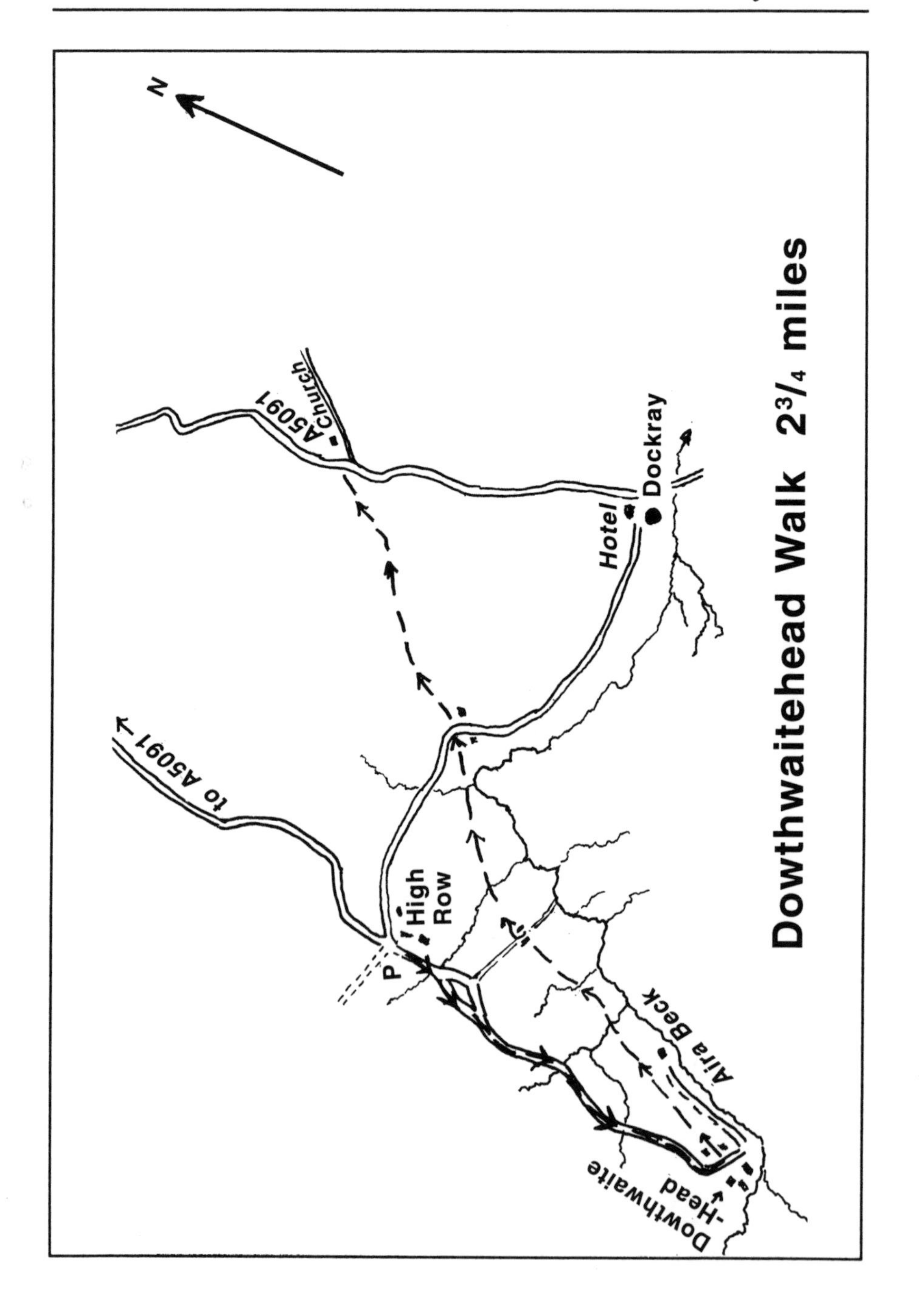
N
A5091
Church
to A5091
Dockray
Hotel
High Row
P
Aira Beck
Dowthwaite-Head
Dowthwaitehead Walk $2^3/_4$ miles

and pass a house named 'Borrowscale'.

4. As you enter the hamlet the road turns left before its end. Look for a finger post directing you left on to a field path.

5. Leave the road and go along a marked track to a gate. Proceed along the side of a fence to another gate.

6. Walk along the side of a wall, keeping clear of the wettest places.

7. From here the walk is fairly straight, going across several fields through gates.

8. The path is not so clear but make for a stone stile through the wall. Ahead of you there is a collection of buildings.

9. Cross the road and turn left around the buildings on the other side. From here the surrounding area is quite rugged as the path passes near the beck.

10. Continue to cross fields through gates until a slight rise in the path brings you to another road.

11. Cross the road. A finger post directs you on your way around the side of the building.

12. The path leads you to cross a number of fields but you are guided by a wall on your right. When you leave its shelter there is a path going off to the right. Ignore this and go straight ahead towards a collection of buildings.

13. You have reached a Field Centre and are directed down to the main road.

14. Turn left on the road for a few yards. Pass the church on the corner and go to a lay-by on the left side of the road. This is the picking-up point.

12. Hartsop to Patterdale

Length of walk: $2^1/_2$ miles

Map ref: NY 410131 (Outdoor Leisure Map No 5)

Starting height: 650ft (198.1 m)

Finishing height: 480ft (146.3 m)

Hartsop is a sleepy, peaceful village, with friendly and helpful inhabitants. On the walk, views of fells to the west and south are exciting. There are glimpses into the valleys of Dovedale, Deepdale and, further on, Grisedale. To the north gleams the southern curve of Ullswater, and on the eastern side, a 'there and back' walk to Silver Crag which may tempt you another time.

Driver

The dropping point is in Hartsop Village. The A592 runs the length of Kirkstone Pass – south towards Windermere and north to Patterdale. The turn off to Hartsop is at a sharp bend within sight of Brothers Water, well signposted. The parking area is through the village.

Reaching the picking-up point entails returning to the main A592 road, turning right, and going towards Patterdale. There are several possible parking places in and around the village.

The Walk

Spinning Gallery. Hartsop.

1. Leave the car park and walk back towards the village. There is a finger post pointing to the right. A gate bars the way with a sign pointing to Rathmore.

2. Go through the gate and start a slight ascent for about 50 yards. At the top of the incline the ground is much more loose underfoot.

3. From here, the path is well-defined and flat. Time should be taken to look back at the fine views of surrounding fells and of Brothers Water.

4. Paths join from both sides, but press on. By the side of a house is a short narrow passage with a stile at each end. Over the second stile you go on to the open fell.

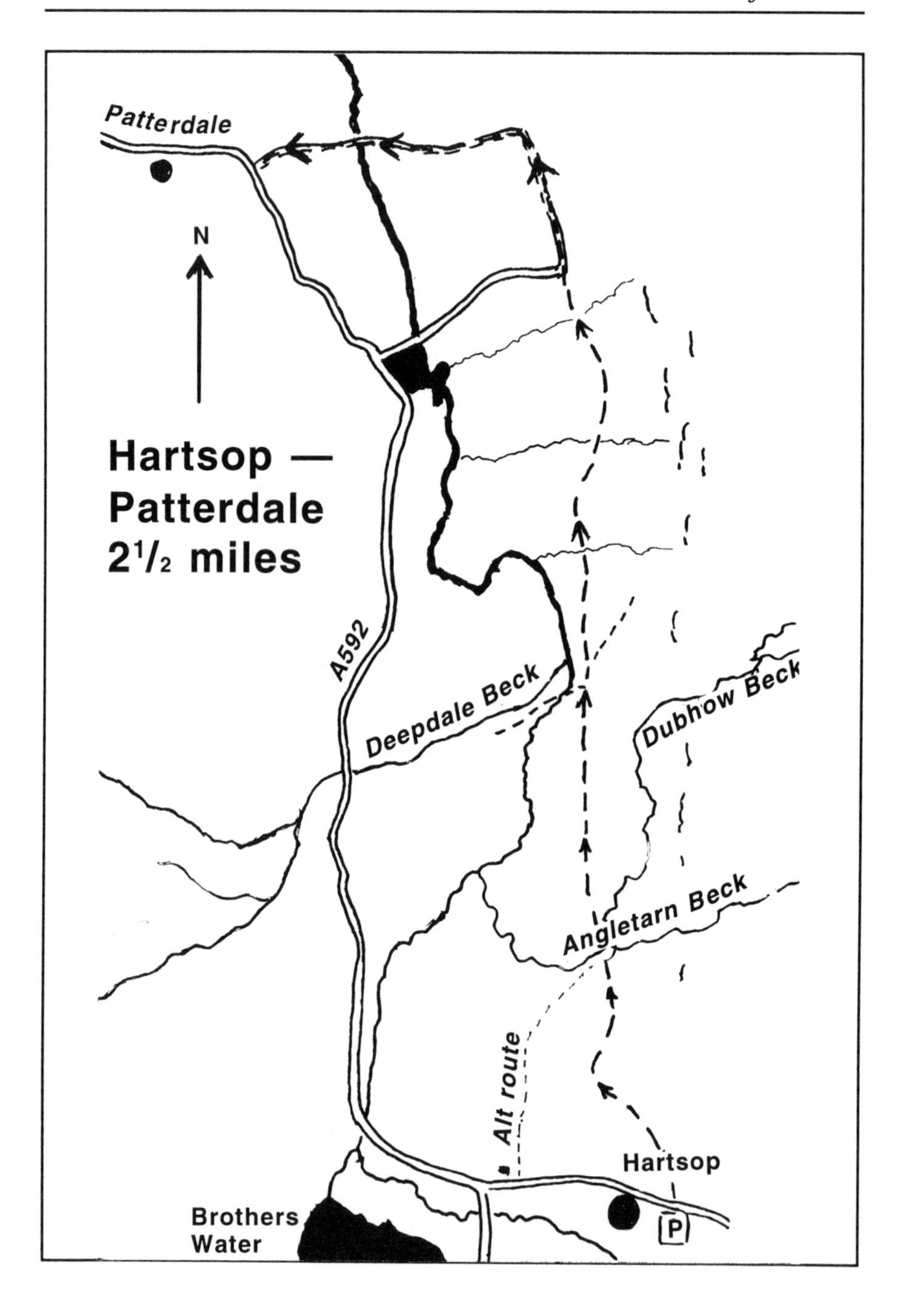
Patterdale
N
Hartsop —
Patterdale
2½ miles
A592
Deepdale Beck
Dubhow Beck
Angletarn Beck
Alt route
Hartsop
P
Brothers
Water

5. This part of the walk can be quite wet. You may need to walk on 'stepping stones' but beware, wet stones or rocks can be slippery.

6. Where the wall you have been walking by turns up the fell, there is a stile. Climb it and turn immediately down the side of the wall to a wooden bridge. Cross the beck.

7. This is a fine spot to linger awhile, watching the water tumbling down Angletarn Beck.

8. Ignore the path going up the fellside. Further on there is another path junction – left to Deepdale Bridge. You go straight ahead.

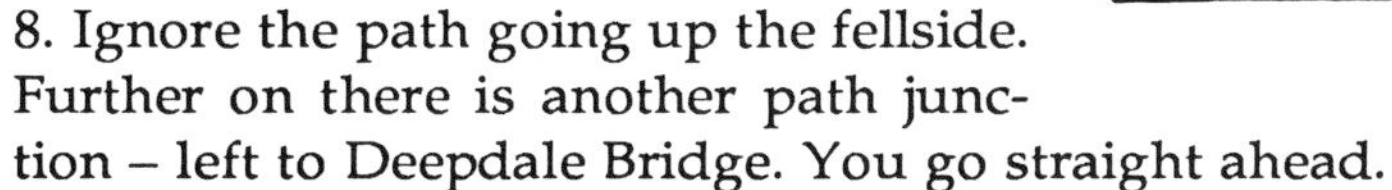

9. There is a slight rise in the path as you walk towards a small plantation, then a gentle descent to a small hamlet.

10. Turn left on to a tarmacadam single track road, over a bridge and on to the A592 road as it enters Patterdale.

Alternative route:

1. For those who may find the first 50 yards of the walk too arduous, walk back through the village and almost down to the main A592 road.

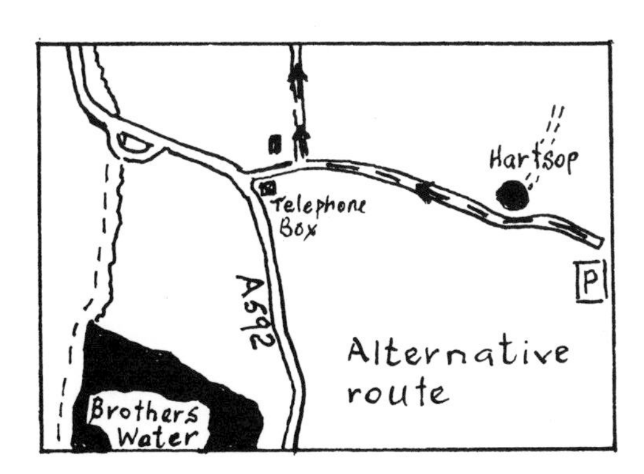

2. Turn right at an Outdoor Centre building. There is a sign on the wall pointing the way along a bridle path.

3. This is a level walk, nevertheless one to be enjoyed for its openness and fine fell views.

4. Cross Edge Beck and walk by a scattering of trees until you reach a gate. Through this is Angletarn Beck.

5. The rest of the walk is as from (7) in the main directions.

13. Kirkstone to Brothers Water

Length of walk: $2^3/_4$ miles

Map ref: NY 403089 (Outdoor Leisure Map No 5 & 7)

Starting height: 1300ft (396.3 m)

Finishing height: 480ft (146.3 m)

If travelling from Ambleside or Windermere you may spot the large rock on the left of the road that, as Wordsworth said, "gives to the savage pass its name". The Kirk Stone is to be found about five hundred yards north of the Kirkstone Pass Inn. Near Red Screes, shouting may be heard. Unless it is of alarm, it most certainly will be people testing out the good echo conditions created by the towering fells.

As you leave the road at the beginning of the walk any noise made by car or man is soon dampened by distance and the sound of running water.

Driver

The dropping-off point is at a parking area situated about 1000 yards to the north of the Kirkstone Pass Inn on the A592. The parking area is clearly marked as you approach it from either Patterdale in the north or Windermere to the south.

To reach the picking-up point, go down the pass towards Patterdale. Just past the end of Brothers Water the road bends to the left and 400 yards further on there is another parking sign. There is plenty of parking space on either side of Cow Bridge. This is the picking-up point.

The Walk

1. There is a stile at the corner of the car park. Go over this and on to the fell side. There is a path just visible going down parallel to the road.

2. There is a very good view of Brothers Water and the fells beyond. Just past a wall on the left you join a path leading from the road.

3. Continue on the path which runs by the side of Kirkstone Beck. As the path turns, away from road and beck and around the lower slopes of Middle Dodd it turns into a pleasant grassy walk.

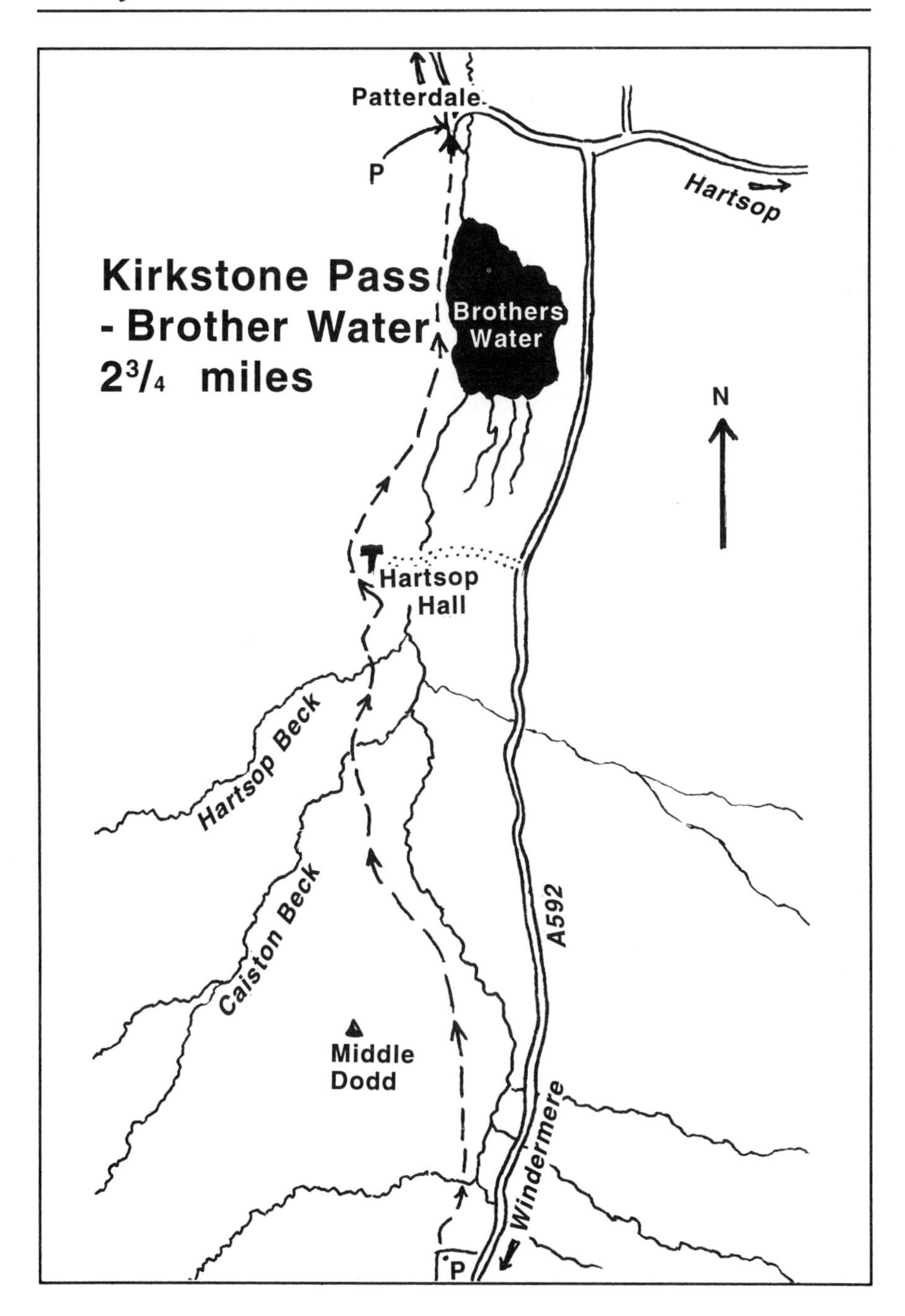
Patterdale
P
Hartsop
Kirkstone Pass
- Brother Water
2¾ miles
Brothers
Water
N
Hartsop
Hall
Hartsop Beck
Caiston Beck
A592
Middle
Dodd
Windermere
P

4. The path continues to curve away from the road and through a number of field walls. It takes you to a small bridge where two walls meet at right angles to each other. Cross the bridge over Caiston Beck, and up a slight incline straight ahead where you will join a path coming from a wicket gate to your left.

5. Turn to the right and go by a stone wall to an old barn. Go through the small yard and on to meadow land with well marked path.

6. The path takes you to farm buildings. When reached, turn right on edge of the field to a stile. Climb the stile then go over a small wooden bridge, and so on to a farm road.

7. The building ahead is Hartsop Hall. Turn round the left side of the buildings and go through a gate on to a wide and well-trodden farm track.

8. The path continues along the side of Brothers Water to Cow Bridge and so to the car park, your picking-up point.

14. Latrigg

Length of walk: 2.4 miles

Map ref: NY 282254 (Outdoor Leisure Map No 4)

Starting height: 940ft (286.5 m)

Finishing height: 487ft (148.5 m)

Visitors to Keswick cannot fail to notice the fell immediately to the north of the town. Many walk its height to view the lakes and range of fells in the area. From Station Street, in the town, little figures can usually be seen ranged along Latrigg's long summit. People choosing binoculars or cameras in the chemist's shop there try the lenses out by turning to Latrigg.

This walk begins in a sheltered area to the north of the fell. In a very short time a point is reached where there is a full skyline of shapes and peaks that need time, and a clear day for their examination. A bonus lies to the east, for here can often be seen a faint outline of the Pennines, beyond Penrith.

The sight of the old railway, now a recognised walk, can be a sadness to those who cherished the steam age, but a joy to the botanist and to those who seek quietness.

Driver

At the traffic roundabout on the Keswick A66 bypass, turn on to the A591 Carlisle Road. Almost immediately turn right by a caravan site. Go up the road past the Underscar Hotel. A sign directs you up a very narrow road to Skiddaw. At the top of the road there is a car park, the dropping point.

Go back to the A66 and travel east for $3^1/_2$ miles. Turn off right at a road sign "Stone Circle" and "St John's in the Vale". Two hundred yards on is a stone bridge beside a small house. This is your picking-up point.

The Walk

1. Leave the car park and walk on through the gate in the fence at the head of the road. Go straight ahead on a grassy, sometimes wet, path.

2. After passing through a fence the path heads to the corner of the woods. Go down the side of the trees to its end.

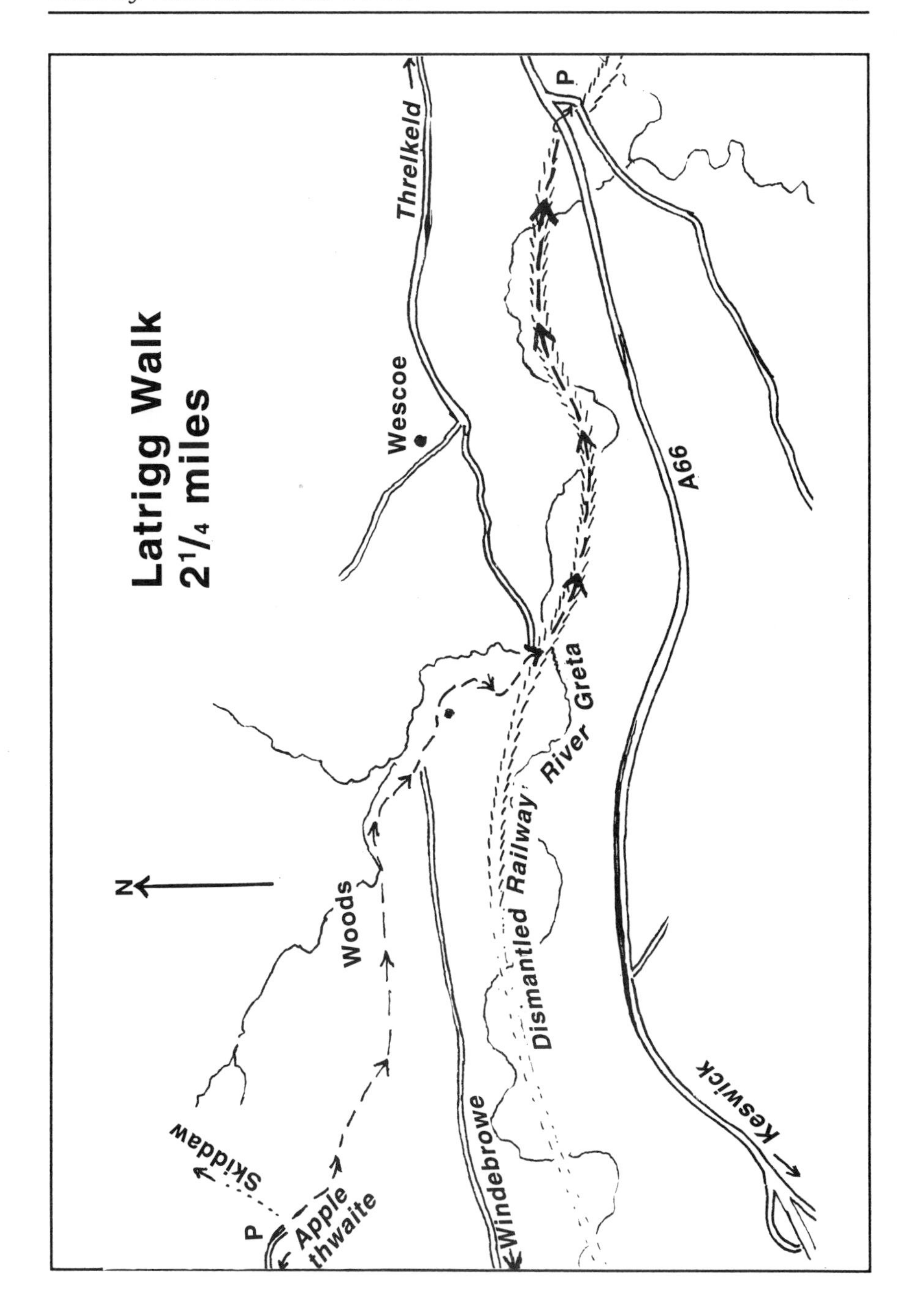
Latrigg Walk
2¼ miles
N
Threlkeld
Wescoe
A66
River Greta
Dismantled Railway
Woods
Skiddaw
P
Apple thwaite
Windebrowe
Keswick
P

3. The wide path then crosses open grazing land. There are excellent views of the lake, Borrowdale Valley and the north west fells.

4. Go through the gate on to the lane. Turn left then bear right as it falls away. The Glenderaterra Beck is on your left.

5. Walk past a house on the right and continue down a steep part of the lane. Near the bottom, and before reaching a stone bridge, there is a gate on the right.

6. Go through the gate, and through another, 30 yards ahead. You are on the old Penrith to Keswick railway line – now an official walk.

7. Turn left and continue the walk over an old metal bridge. There is still a great deal of railway memorabilia to be seen. Note the rich variety of plants growing on old retaining walls in some of the railway cuttings.

8. The walk continues along the River Greta. As you near the end of the walk you will see another old metal bridge ahead of you.

9. Just before the bridge a path goes off to the right through a gate. Take that path, it goes under the new A66. Soon you see a stone bridge supporting the original A66.

10. Go through the two gates on to the road. This is your picking-up point. Before embarking, look over the side of the bridge. On the one side is the meeting of two waters – St John's Beck and River Glenderamackin – both of which combine on the other side of the bridge to become the River Greta.

15. Loughrigg to Miller Bridge

Length of walk: $2^3/_4$ miles

Map ref: NY 340056 (Outdoor Leisure Map No 7)

Starting height: 536ft (163.2 m)

Finishing height: 160ft (48.7 m)

On a clear day, reflections in Grasmere, well seen from this promenade, can be stunning, even confusing, so true are they to the scene above. Take your camera, sketch book, mini paint box – or just stand and stare.

The Wordsworths walked this way, not always by the same route, but certainly from Grasmere to Rydal and often on to Ambleside to take or collect their many letters. Then the name in common use for the road under Loughrigg Fell, near the Rothay, was Clappersgate.

An extract from Dorothy's Journal, Friday 16th May, 1800 reads:

> *". . . After tea went to Ambleside – a pleasant cool but not cold evening. Rydal was very beautiful with spear-shaped streaks of polished steel. No letters! – only one newspaper. I returned by Clappersgate. Grasmere was very solemn in the last glimpse of twilight it calls home the heart to quietness".*

Driver

The dropping-off point is on the road linking Grasmere with Skelwith Bridge, on that part called Red Bank. This can be reached by going through Grasmere Village and taking the road down the west side of the lake. Past the end of the lake the road climbs. Just before a fork in the road is reached, there is a gate on the left – the start of the walk.

To reach the picking-up point, go back through Grasmere and take the A591 towards Ambleside. Just beyond Rydal Village there is a turn off on the right. Take this narrow road over a bridge then across open land. After a mile you will see a stone bridge over the river on your left. This is the picking-up point. There is ample, safe parking space at the side of the road.

The Walk

1. Walk back down the road for a few yards and go through the gate on your right. Go down the steep leafy lane.

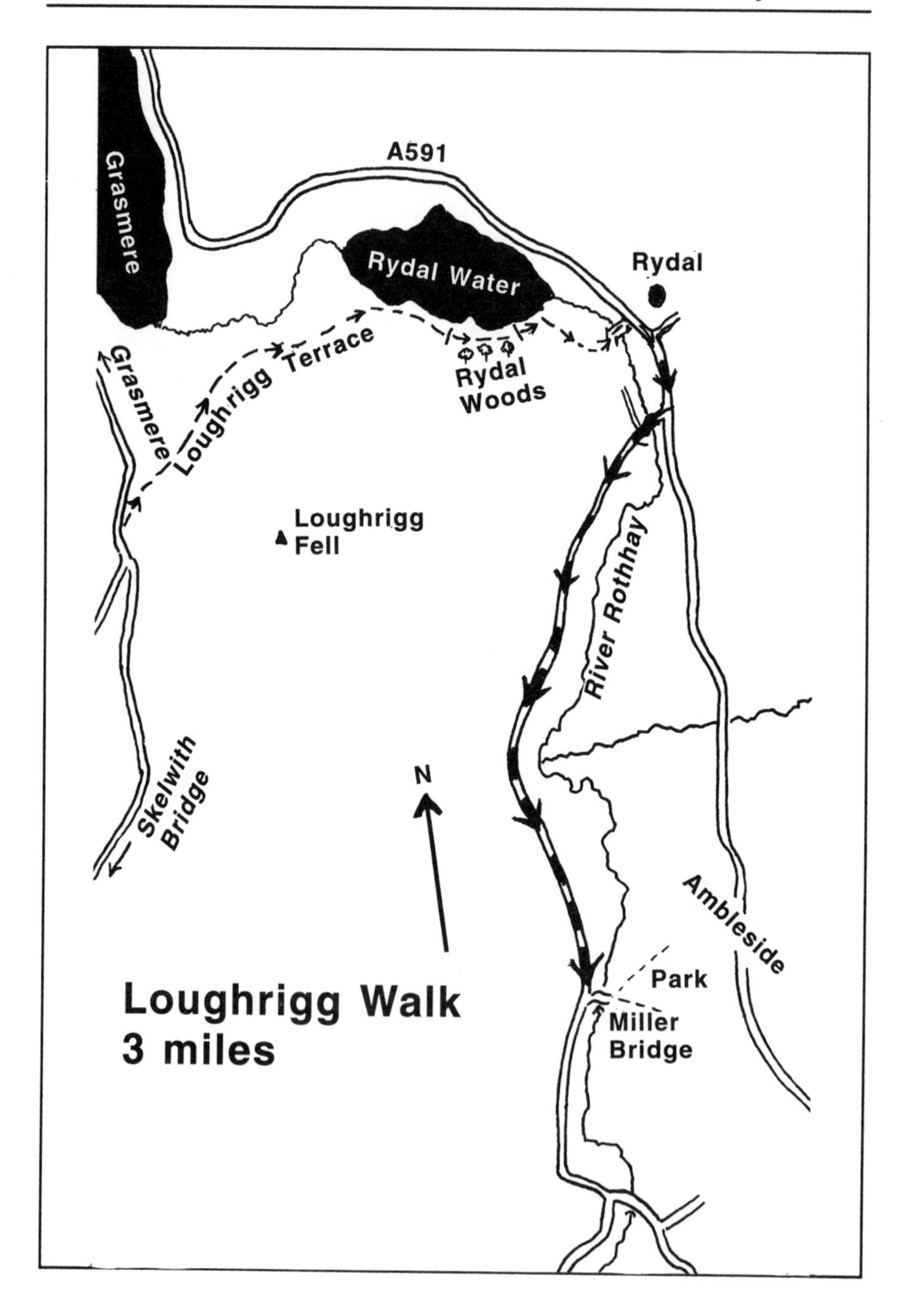
A591
Grasmere
Rydal Water
Rydal
Grasmere
Loughrigg Terrace
Rydal Woods
Loughrigg Fell
River Rothhay
Skelwith Bridge
N
Ambleside
Park
Miller Bridge
Loughrigg Walk
3 miles

2. The path curves round the foot of Loughrigg Fell. You will come to a meeting of paths. Ignore the steeply descending one to the left and go straight ahead.

3. The path crosses a stream. Pause awhile to take in the splendour of Grasmere and the fells beyond.

4. The path follows the side of a wall. Ignore an entry through the wall, and go on, passing a barn on your left.

5. The path descends to the shores of Rydal Water. There is a lot to catch the eye – the islands and the far side of the lake, to the sky line shaped by Nab Scar.

6. Pass through a metal wicket gate into Rydal Woods. Yet another pleasant view presents itself if you turn to look back along the length of Rydal Water.

7. Pass through another metal wicket gate. Go across some rough grazing land to a wooden bridge spanning River Rothay. On reaching the A591 opposite Glen Rothay Hotel, turn right, and walk along the pavement towards Pelter bridge.

8. The bridge is at the head of a road that leaves the A591 to the right. You cross what is almost meadow land until you reach a cattle grid.

9. From here onwards the walk is along the metalled road that runs by the side of River Rothay. There is still a great deal to interest until Miller Bridge, your picking-up point, is reached.

16. Keskadale

Length of walk: 1.6 miles

Map ref: NY 210194 (Outdoor Leisure Map No 4)

Starting height: 787.4ft (240 m)

Finishing height: 390ft (119 m)

For most of the year, this could be called a wet walk – very green, but wet underfoot! Fortunately, the 'downhill' is gradual so, as long as you are well shod, there should not be any anxiety about where-to-put feet.

Field paths usually mean grass and stiles, and for just over half its length that is the nature of this walk. A very pleasant, easy end gives you the time to study surrounding fells. As the eye looks south west over Scope End the larger of Hindscarth's two cairns may be seen. Dale Head lies to the left of Hindscarth and Robinson to the right.

Driver

Leave the A66 for Braithwaite just west of Keswick. In the middle of the village take the left turn to Newlands. The road is quite narrow in places. It passes along the sides of Barrow and Causey Pike. It then crosses over the bridge at Rigg Beck. As you approach the next 'S' bend you will see ahead, Keskadale Farm. Stop on the right at the bottom of the 'S' bend. This is the dropping point.

Turn back towards Braithwaite. Just at the 'S' bend there is a narrow road going down the right side of the purple painted house. Take this road. Down in the valley you will cross a stone bridge. Just over the bridge, and on the right, is a parking place, the picking-up point.

The Walk

1. From the parking area, walk back 25 yards and go through a gate on the other side of the road.

2. There is a finger post pointing your way down the track. The area is quite wet at certain parts of the year so care has to be taken over footwear.

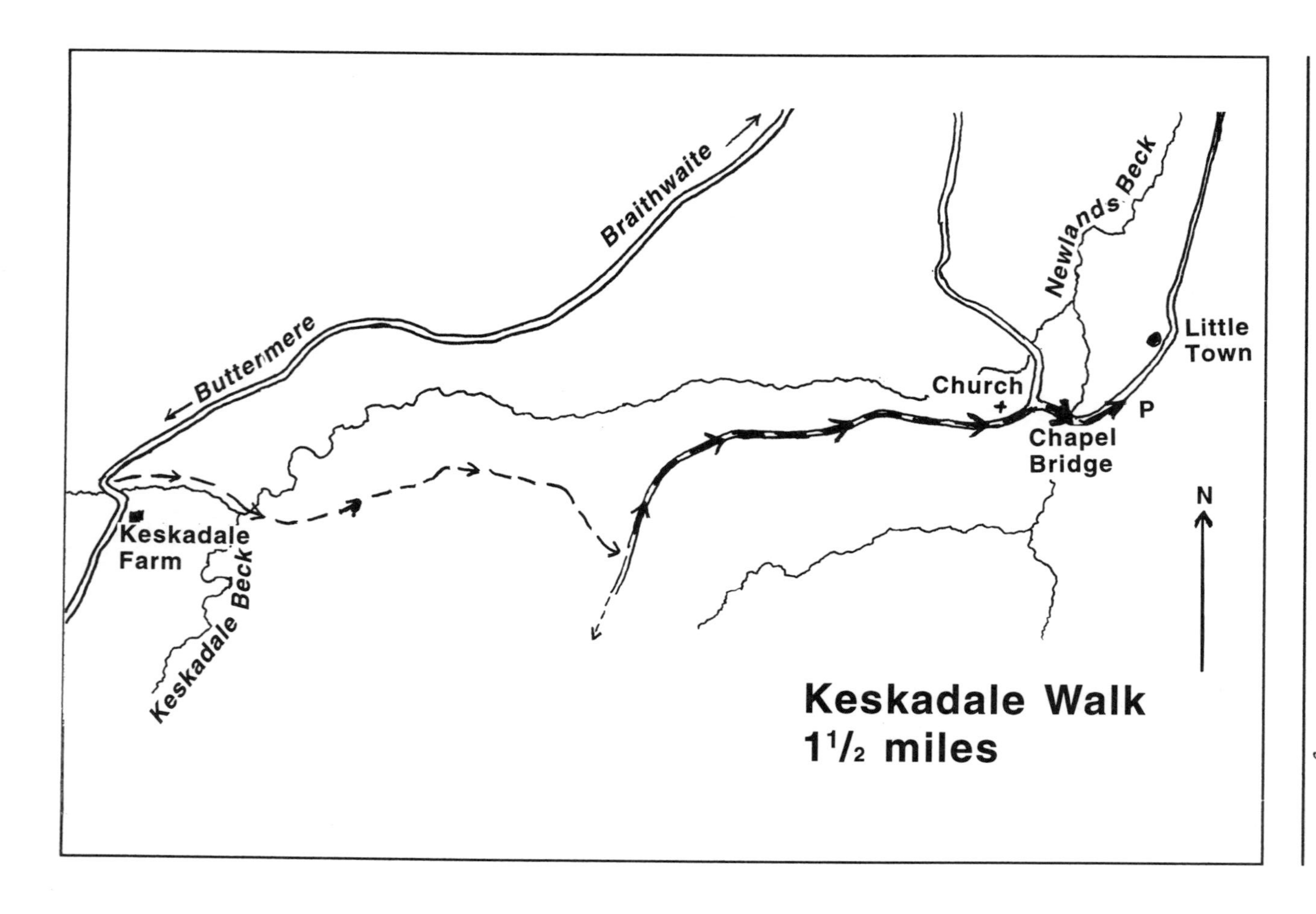
Braithwaite
Buttermere
Newlands Beck
Little Town
Church
P
Chapel Bridge
N
Keskadale Farm
Keskadale Beck
Keskadale Walk
1½ miles

3. Keskadale Farm is up on your right. The area around seems to be rather untidy, but one could say it looks industrious.

4. A path goes away to the left. Ignore it and continue down to the beck. Cross the footbridge.

5. The path now bears to the left through several fields. It runs parallel with the beck in a continuous straight line.

6. The path can be faint in places, possibly due to continuous wetness not allowing permanent scarring.

7. After passing through five fields the path bends to the right and soon meets a path coming from Bawd Hall from the left. The course of the beck has also changed flowing through tree-lined banks.

8. You are directed through two more fields still bearing to the right. The path runs alongside a hedge as it reaches a farm lane.

9. Turn left on the lane. The problems of negotiating gates, stiles and water are now over. While the lane is tree-lined, there are gaps enough to see the fells to the west.

10. You are now in the centre of a circle of imposing fells where ascents can be picked out with the naked eye. Binoculars would make viewing even better.

11. Continue along the lane to the church. Go on through the gate and turn right over the bridge. Your picking-up point is on the right.

17. Little Langdale to Elterwater

Length of walk: $1^3/_4$ miles

Map ref: NY 323035 (Outdoor Leisure Map No 6)

Starting height: 430ft (131.1 m)

Finishing height: 200ft (61 m)

The walk curls around the lower slopes of Lingmoor Fell before reaching the quarries above Chapel Stile. There is the chance to see the spoil of a slate quarry and to note how Nature is beginning to smother the signs of industrial activity. Slate is visible along the whole of the lower part of the walk. In a different way, it is there at the end. Gunpowder Cottage is a holiday home, converted from a building where gunpowder for the mines was stored. See if you can find it.

Driver

To reach the dropping point leave Elterwater Village by the Coniston Road. Turn up Wrynose at High Colwith and continue through Little Landale Village. Just 200 yards past the village is a narrow road to the right leading to Dale End Farm. This is the dropping point.

Return down the road to Elterwater Village. Just over the bridge, and on the right, is a public car park, your picking-up point.

The Walk

1. From the dropping point walk along the lane towards Dale End Farm. The way is slightly uphill but flattens out as the farm is reached.

2. The lane becomes a bridle path now also signposted as a cyclists' track.

3. You will pass a 'public path' sign pointing at right angles across a field on your right. This is a downward path back to Little Langdale Village. Your path, however, is not down the bridle path.

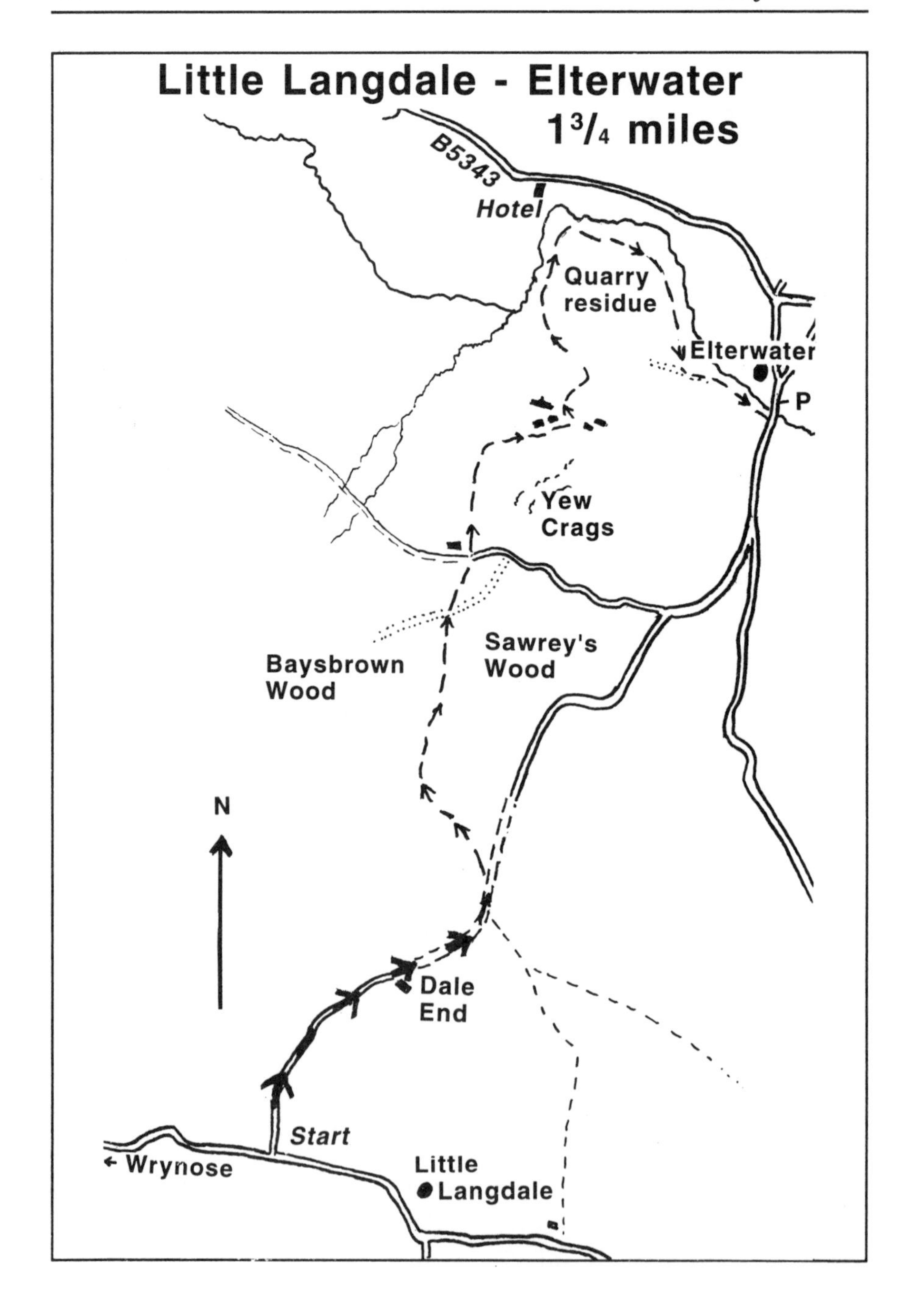
Little Langdale - Elterwater
1¾ miles
B5343
Hotel
Quarry residue
Elterwater
P
Yew Crags
Sawrey's Wood
Baysbrown Wood
N
Dale End
Start
← Wrynose
Little Langdale

4. Just over 200 yards further on, and on the left side, is an entrance into the woods.

5. The path through the woods takes you slightly uphill as it goes round the side of the fell, before turning downhill.

6. Cross a forest track and continue until you arrive on the Baysbrown Farm road.

7. The building you see is Crossgates Cottage. Your way is by the side of the cottage down the wide grassy path.

8. The path takes you to a quarry yard. It is well signposted between the sheds. It then drops down among quarry spoil to the side of Great Langdale Beck.

9. Go along the beck side ignoring the wooden bridge to your left. Soon there is a slight uphill walk to reach a metalled road.

10. The road now takes you downhill to where you meet another road. Turn left for Elterwater Village. Cross the bridge spanning the beck. Your picking-up point is in the car park on the right side of the road.

18. Lower Thirlmere

Length of walk: Nearly 2 miles

Map ref: NY 330111 (Outdoor leisure Map No 5)

Starting height: 700ft (213.4 m)

Finishing height: 590ft (179.8 m)

Dunmail Raise squeezes through that space left between Steel Fell and Seat Sandal. The very narrowness helps to draw your attention ahead to Thirlmere and the forest on its eastern side. There is a ruggedness about parts of the walk that demands concentration; in any standing and staring, particularly at waterfalls, first secure your 'standing'.

Driver

The dropping point is on the A591 north of Grasmere. From the village, the road starts to climb as you pass the Travellers' Rest. As the road flattens out on the brow of Dunmail Raise, you will see a stone building and an AA box on the right. Just a few yards further on, there is a lay-by, the dropping point.

To reach the picking-up point, go northwards. As the road descends you will see the lake ahead. Just about 400 yards from its start there is a turning off to the right, a very rough, wide track. Go up the track for about 50 yards to a car park, the picking-up point.

The Walk

1. Go forward to the stile. Cross into the field and turn left. The grass is tussocky and rather hard to walk on.

2. Keep near to the road. You will pass two stiles leading to the road, ignore them.

3. At the second stile you will notice a broad green path going towards and up the fell side. Ignore this also. Cross it and head for a stile in the wall ahead.

4. The path now goes away diagonally from the road. It rounds the top of a wall and you walk by this down to a gill.

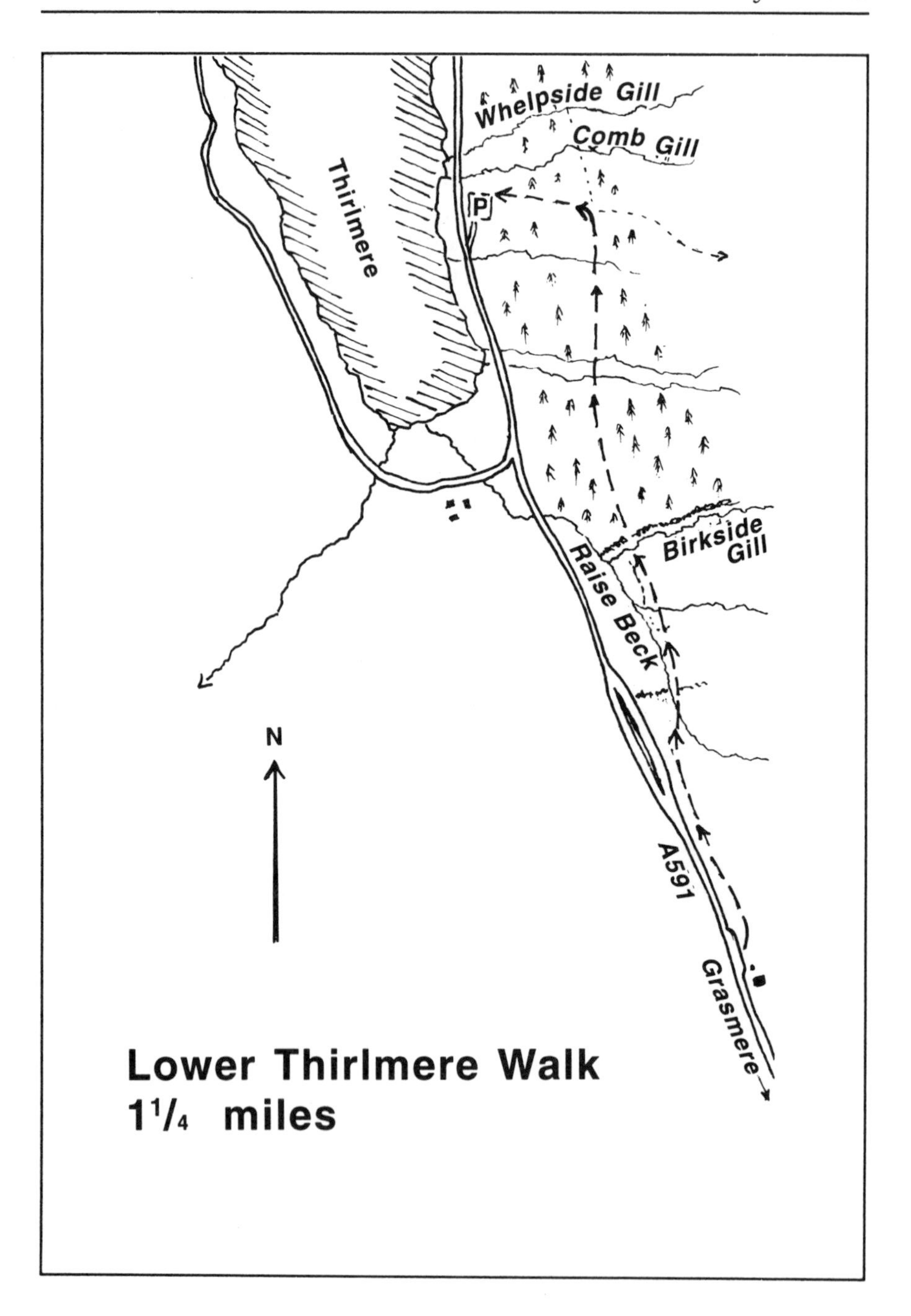

Lower Thirlmere Walk
1¼ miles

5. There is usually a good flow of water tumbling down Birkside Gill. Maps show 'waterfalls' and they are there up above you. Cross the gill by the bridge.

6. having dropped down to the gill, you now need to ascend to the entrance to the woods. The path continues upwards gradually for a while.

7. There are occasional views of the lake and fells on its western side. The path takes you over two unnamed gills.

8. You will eventually reach a finger post with a path going downhill towards the lake.

9. Go down the path but take care because of unevenness of the ground and slipperiness due to running water. The path now goes down the side of Comb Gill.

10. As you near the end of the walk the path is quite rocky. However, going through the newly constructed wicket gate in the wall will bring you to the car park, your picking-up point.

11. Before leaving, visit the church and churchyard. The church is one of the very few buildings left of the village of Wythburn after Thirlmere became a reservoir.

19. Scales to Threlkeld

Length of walk: $2^1/_2$ miles

Map ref: NY 342268 (Outdoor Leisure Map No 5)

Starting height: 725ft (221 m)

Finishing height: 450ft (137.2 m)

There is no village at Scales. The area is nevertheless a busy one for parking and walking. Along the nearby A66 every lay-by and bit of old road is used for walkers' cars, but the choice of paths is so great that people quickly become dispersed on their way to the tops.

The further you walk away from Scales the more you can see of Blencathra's five vast fells – learn them off by heart and recall them in you mind's eye on bleak days in the office! To the south is the large, sloping Threlkeld Common and the hill which forms the extreme northern end of the Helvellyn range, Clough Head.

Driver

The dropping-off point is on the loop road passing the door of the White Horse Inn. The inn is situated just off the A66 – six miles east of Keswick and twelve miles west of Penrith. The loop road is quiet compared with the main trunk road.

To reach the picking-up point, go on towards Keswick for $2^1/_2$ miles then turn left on the B5322. Go down this road for just less than half a mile where there is a sharp left turn on to a narrow road sign-posted to Threlkeld Quarry. There is parking space in sight of the rows of houses and beside an old bridge on your left. The bridge straddles a dismantled railway cutting and leads to a farmyard. This is your picking-up point.

The Walk

1. From the White Horse go to the A66 and turn towards Keswick. About 40 yards down on the left side of the road, opposite an old house, you will see a stile.

2. Cross the road carefully then climb the stile. Walk down by the wall until another stile is reached.

3. Once over the stile turn right and follow the fence to a tree, then strike off diagonally across the open field until you meet another wire fence.

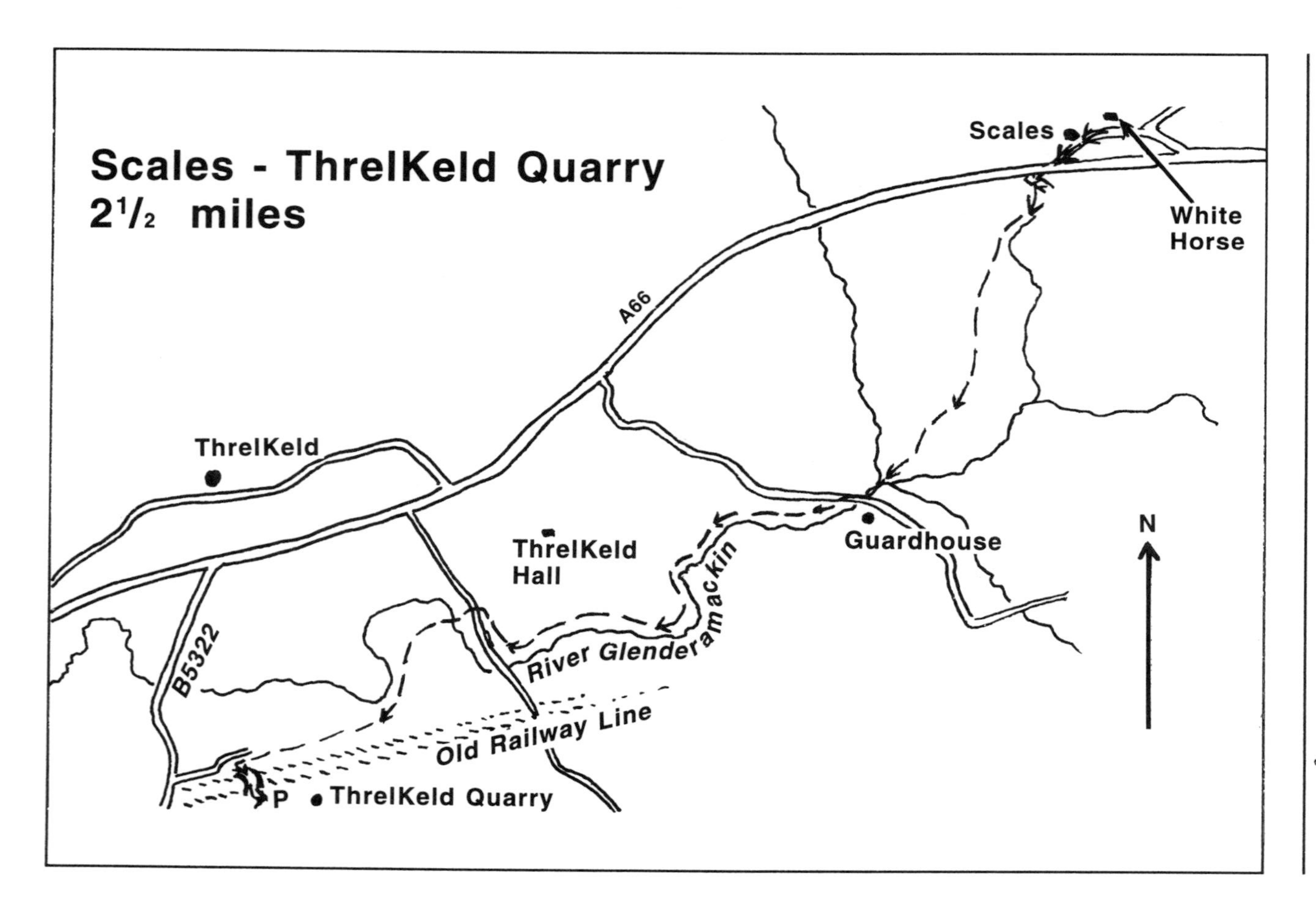
Scales - ThrelKeld Quarry
2 1/2 miles
Scales
White Horse
A66
ThrelKeld
ThrelKeld Hall
Guardhouse
N
River Glenderamackin
B5322
Old Railway Line
P
ThrelKeld Quarry

4. Turn left at the fence until you reach another stile. Looking back the way you have come gives you a very good view of Blencathra.

5. Cross over the stile and continue diagonally across the field aiming for the edge of the line of trees. From here the path goes to the right towards the end of a broken-down wall.

6. The stile ahead leads on to very wet land – note the reeds. If, instead, you take the stile to your left, and follow the fence around, you will arrive at the same spot – much dryer.

7. On reaching the road you will see the hamlet of Guardhouse to your left. Turn to the right and seek a finger post directing you to Threlkeld. Follow the path over a wooden bridge and along the river side.

8. A small gated bridge astride a stream is crossed and a more open path is followed along the river bank with a view of Keswick Golf Course on the far bank.

9. A stile is reached at the edge of a copse and the path leads to a narrow road. Cross over the bridge to the left then over a stile to the right.

10. The path bears away to the left, away from the river. It crosses a stream over a tiny bridge.

11. The path meets the river again and a farm track is reached. As you near the first of the farm buildings turn left and across an old railway bridge. The picking-up point is on the other side of the bridge.

20. Loweswater

Length of walk: $2^1/_2$ miles

Map ref: NY 106226 (Outdoor Leisure Map No 4)

Starting height: 715ft (218 m)

Finishing height: 410ft (125 m)

Loweswater, being on the edge of the National Park, attracts fewer visitors and retains a quiet air.

From the start of the walk to the lakeside there are signs and sounds of agricultural Lakeland – animal noises, farm noises, and around, there are squat farm buildings, and all set amid fells with lovely names – Burnbank Fell, Carling Knott, Darling Fell and Bield. The fall of land to the shore of the lake offers some protection to its placid waters. Reflections of white painted houses and the odd, coloured boat are mental images to take away with you.

Driver

Take the B5289 (Cockermouth to Buttermere) road and turn where directed to Loweswater. You pass the village and soon reach the lake on its northern side. Continue along the road until you reach a road junction. Go on to the left passing Fangs Brow Farm. About 100 yards past the farm there is a lay-by with a finger post directing through a gate. This is the dropping point.

To reach the picking-up point, go back towards Loweswater Village. After you pass the bottom of the lake look for a narrow road on your right with no signpost other than a finger post saying 'Public Footpath'. Go down this narrow road until, at its end, you turn right into a National Trust Car Park. This is the picking-up point.

The Walk

1. Go through the gate with its directions to 'Loweswater' and 'Old Corpse Road', and walk straight ahead on the wide path.

2. Leave the Old Corpse Road and go to your left over the ladder stile.

3. The grassy path starts to go downwards alongside a wall on your right. As you turn-round the side of the fell the lake comes into view.

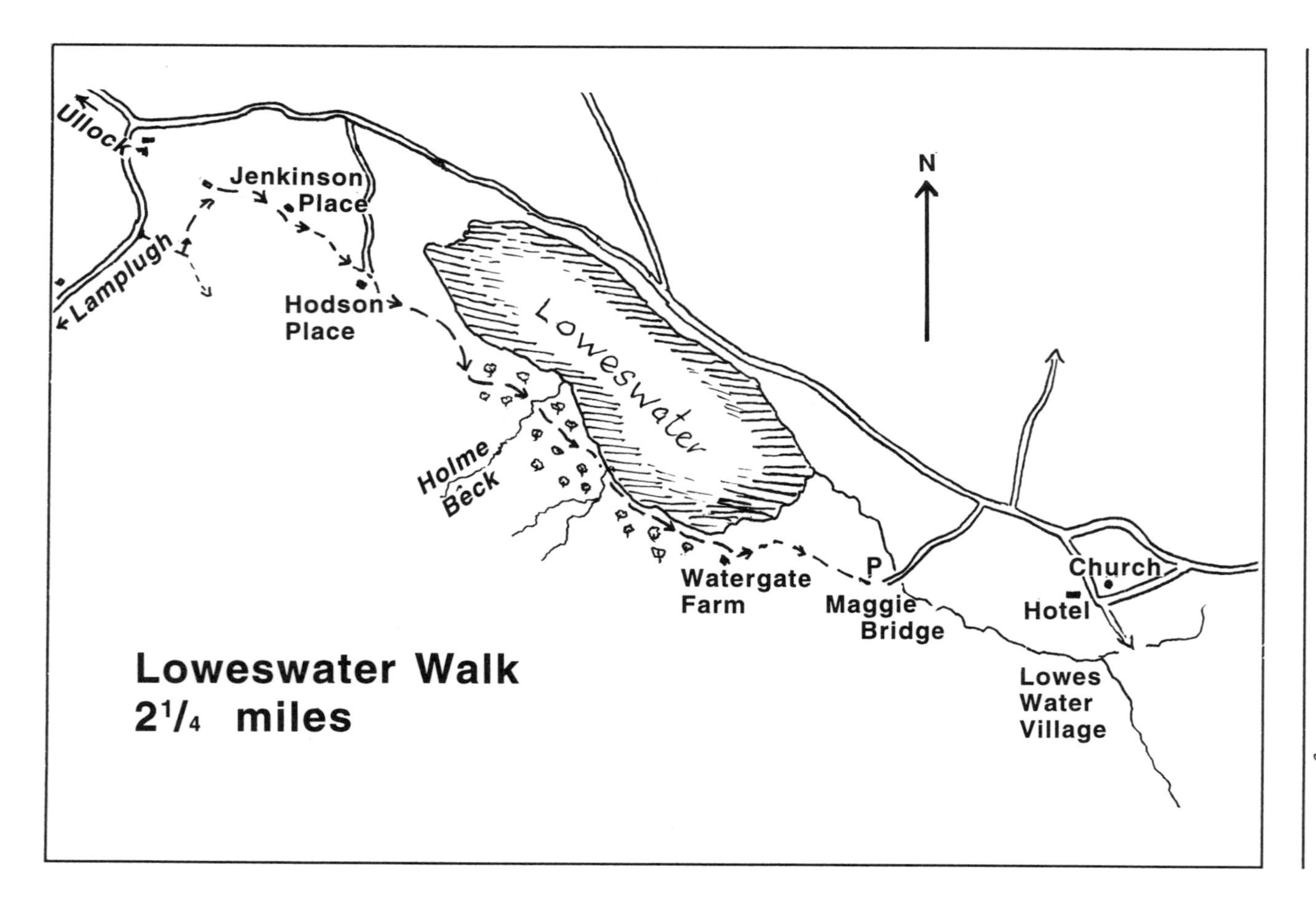
Ullock
Jenkinson
Place
Lamplugh
Hodson
Place
N
Loweswater
Holme
Beck
Watergate
Farm
P
Maggie
Bridge
Church
Hotel
Lowes
Water
Village
Loweswater Walk
2 1/4 miles

4. The path takes you above Iredale Place. The farm track comes in from the left. You will join it and continue straight on.

5. The path then passes above Jenkinson Place, another farm. The way is well signed with little path posts and their yellow arrows.

6. Go over a stile on to a grassy path downwards towards the lake. You will walk through fields on a grassy path towards Hudson Place, where the path can vanish under mud at times.

7. Through the farm you will walk on to a bridle path that continues almost to the lakeside.

8. Through another wicket gate you enter Holme Wood.

9. The way now continues through the woods, a pleasant saunter, crossing Holme Beck and passing along the lakeside.

10. At the far end of the wood Watergate Farm comes into view on your right.

11. Turn left on to the farm track. You will pass over three cattle grids before reaching the car park, your picking-up point.

21. Newlands Hause to Mill Beck

Length of walk: $1^1/_2$ miles

Map ref: NY 193177 (Outdoor Leisure Map No 4)

Starting height: 780ft (237.7 m)

Finishing height: 390ft (118.9 m)

The Hause is a popular spot for car users. Parking is easy. People can dip into the fells here, scrambling up to Moss Force, walking the lower slopes of Knott Rigg for a better view westwards, or just sitting at a height, in refreshing air.

This is a walk where, unusually, the further down you go the wider the vista ahead becomes. Buttermere Village, below is one of the more popular spots of the northern part of the Lake District. From a height it is interesting to see the ant-like figures in and around the village and on crossings between the two lakes. More interesting perhaps, is spotting parties of walkers on the far sky line walking the ridge from High Pike to Red Pike.

Driver

To reach the dropping point leave the A66 west of Keswick and go through Portinscale. The second turn to the right is the road to Buttermere. Travel along this road through Swinside, then just past Stair, turn left on to a road from Braithwaite. From here travel another $3^1/_2$ miles to the head of the valley. You will see a waterfall on the left as the road turns. The dropping point is on the right.

Go straight ahead down the steep but scenic road until you come to a road junction. Turn right and pass the Bridge Hotel. Travel on for about 400 yards and you will see a car park on your left, the picking-up point.

Moss Force

The Walk

1. Despite its short length this walk must be one of the most exciting and exhilarating. Across from the parking area is the waterfall of Moss Beck. then there is the closeness of the fells – Knott Rigg, Whiteless Pike and Robinson.

2. Just at the edge of the parking area is a finger post. It points upwards to Knott Rigg. This is not your way. Walk

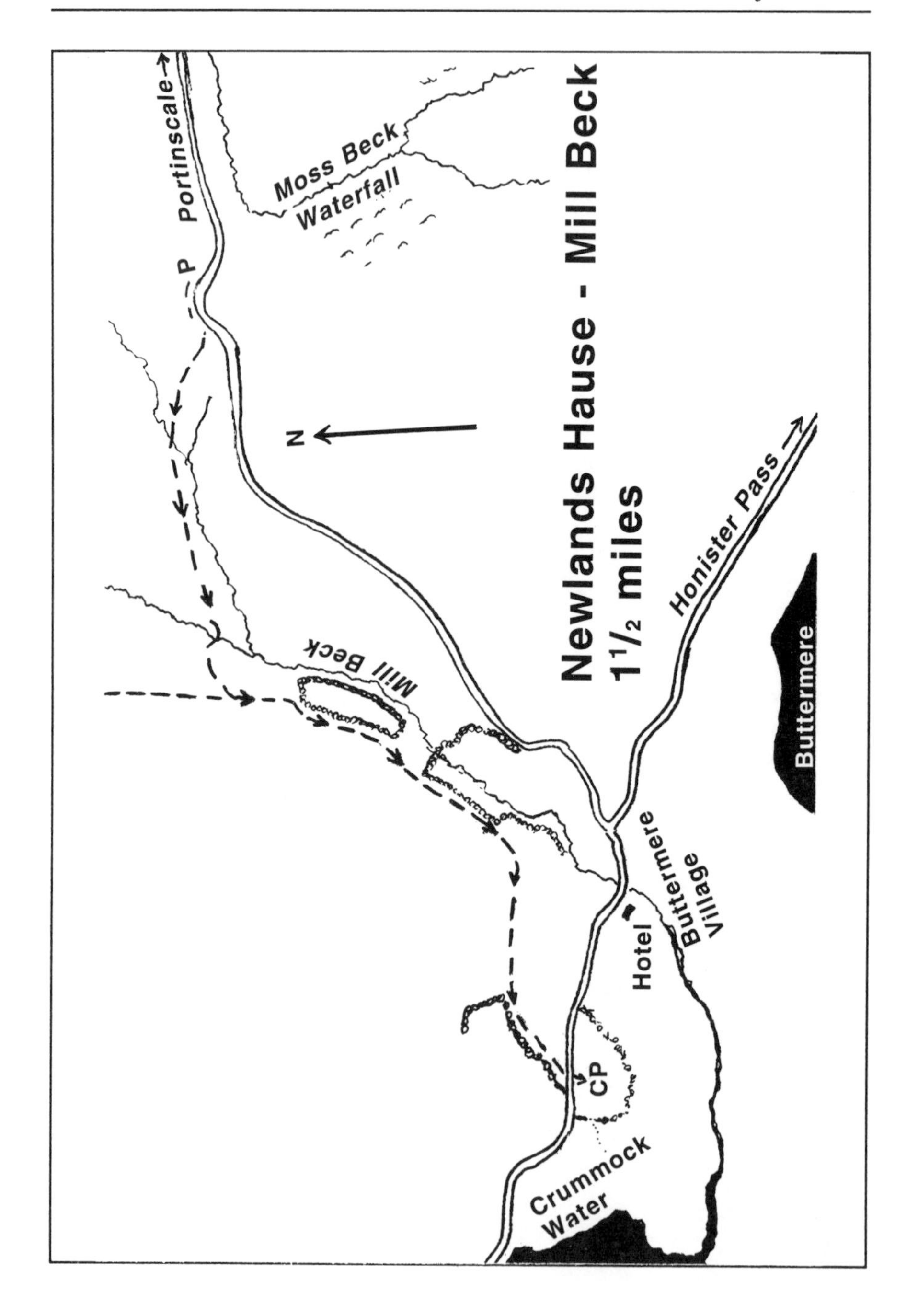

Newlands Hause - Mill Beck
1½ miles
Portinscale
P
Moss Beck
Waterfall
N
Mill Beck
Honister Pass
Buttermere
Buttermere Village
Hotel
CP
Crummock Water

on along the grass verge past the post for 50 yards until you see over the side of the pass.

3. As you begin the walk there is a glimpse of Crummock Water, and Mellbreak and Blea Crag to the west.

4. below, running from right to left is Mill Beck. Your way down to it is by a grassy path running alongside a smaller beck, Swinside Gill.

5. Cross over Mill Beck and walk the few feet uphill to a path that is running parallel with the beck.

6. Turn down the path. The beck is left as enclosing walls block its view.

7. Another wall is reached. From here you can see Buttermere and, far over, Red Pike and High Stile.

8. At the end of the wall, ignore paths off to the left and continue moving to the right.

9. The path meets a wall and continues down its side to the road.

10. The car park on the other side of the road is your picking-up point. If time permits, go through the gate in the car park and spend time wandering down to the mouth of Mill Beck as it enters Crummock Water.

22. Naddle Fell

Length of walk: $2^1/_2$ miles

Map ref: NY 307225 (Outdoor Leisure Map No 4)

Starting height: 710ft (216.4 m)

Finishing height: 550ft (167.5 m)

St John's Church (in the Vale) is isolated, but well-attended. Adjacent is a thriving centre for active visitors to the area. Built in the 1840s, on the site of an earlier church, it has in its burial ground one of the main instigators of its being built, a Cumberland poet, John Richardson.

As the walk is to the south you are viewing part of the Helvellyn range. Clough Head lies to the east, and Calfhow Pike and other lower heights draw your eyes to the narrow and steep valley enclosing Thirlmere.

Driver

From the north, the dropping point is reached by leaving the A66 at Threlkeld, and travelling down the B5322 for $1^1/_4$ miles in the Vale of St John, or from the south it is reached by leaving the A591 at the north end of Thirlmere and on to the B5322 for $2^1/_2$ miles. At a turning to the west at Wanthwaite Bridge travel a quarter of a mile then left again on to a road directing you to St. John's Church. The church is the dropping-off point.

To reach the picking-up point you need to drive back to the B5322 where you turn right and travel for $2^1/_4$ miles. On the right there is a parking area – courtesy of the Wàter Board – a good spot to wait.

The Walk

1. The way starts east of the church over a stile by a gate, sign-posted 'St John's in the Vale'.

2. The path leads downwards past a ruin, Rake How, on the left.

3. You continue with the wall on your left and through a number of gates along a grassy path.

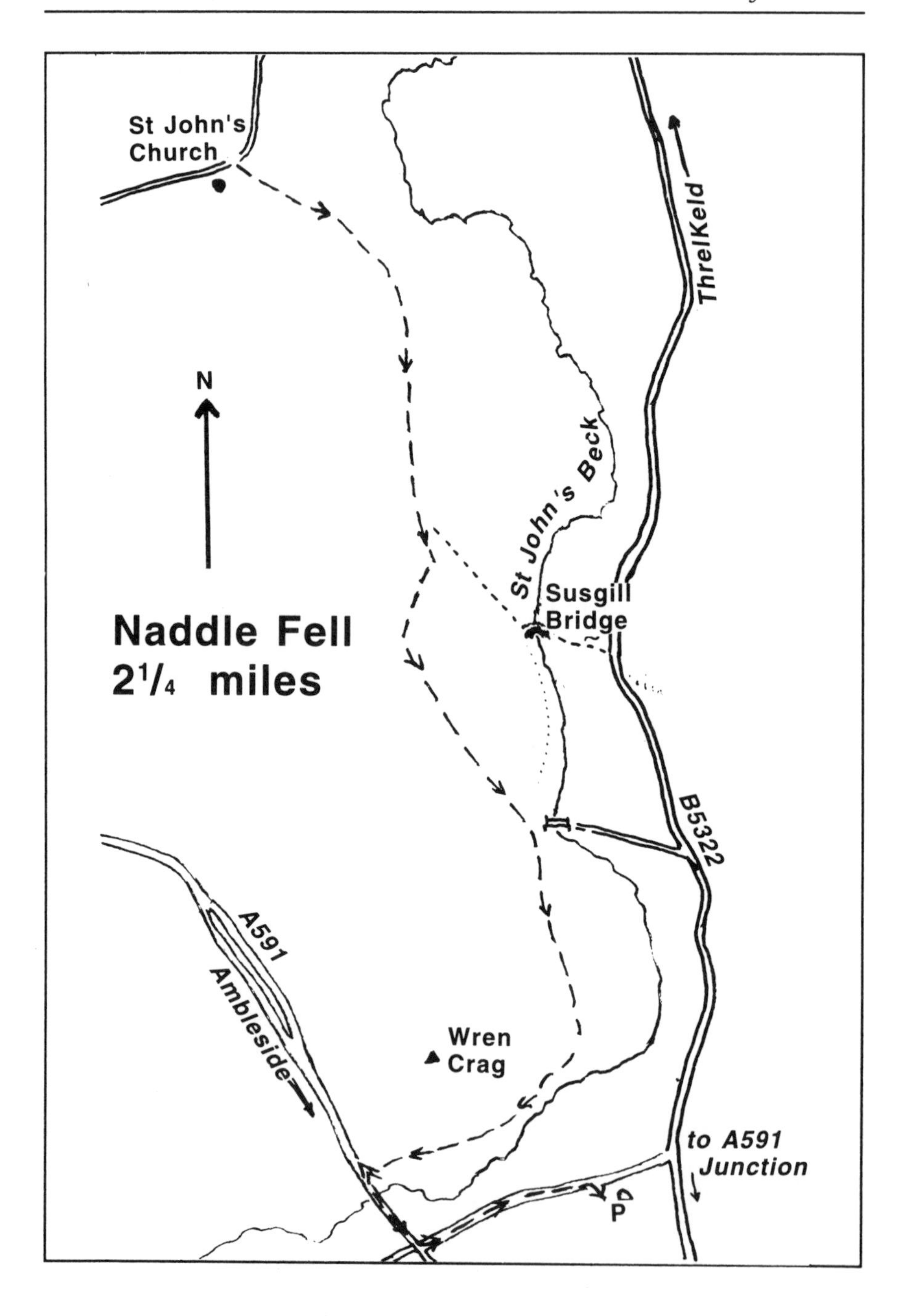
St John's Church
Threlkeld
N
St John's Beck
Susgill Bridge
Naddle Fell
2 1/4 miles
B5322
A591
Ambleside
Wren Crag
to A591 Junction
P

4. You arrive at a wicket gate in the wall. It is here that you can continue on the path by the wall – or – through the wicket gate, walk diagonaliy across to a plank bridge, and on to the flood embankment on the river's edge to a stone humped-backed bridge, 'Sosgill Bridge'.

5. Having visited the bridge, go over the stile and continue along the river's edge until you regain the main path at Low Bridge End Farm.

6. The path continues by the wall past the farm and down to the river's edge. There is a good view of Castle Rock of Triermain ahead.

7. Continue along the river's edge, then you come to a monkey of an incline that takes you to meet the Naddle Fell high walk path.

8. Continue to the stile and on to the main A591 road.

9. Turn left for a few yards then left again on to an old road. A picnic area is passed on the left. It is but a few yards further on to the car park on the right.

23. Rydal

Length of walk: Nearly $2^1/_2$ miles

Map ref: NY 347067 (Outdoor Leisure Map No 7)

Starting height: 455ft (138.5 m)

Finishing height: 160ft (48.7 m)

Literary associations colour this walk. William Wordsworth lived in Dove Cottage for seven and a half years. He did his best work there. After living in other rented property in Grasmere he was able to move into his last home, Rydal Mount, on May 1st 1813, and lived there until his death in 1850. Dorothy, William's sister wrote to her friend, Jane Marshall, '. . . *the place is a paradise* . . . '

It is not generally known that Wordsworth was a good planner of gardens. He was, particularly, a tree man. If there is time, it is worth visiting Rydal Mount, the landscaping there is all his. None of this walk should be hurried.

Driver

Leave the A591 at Grasmere and turn into the side road that runs past Dove Cottage. Continue up the road until you reach rough common land with a duck pond at the side. Do not go on to White Moss but turn left up the side of the rough land to its top. A road goes to the left. Ignore this and carry on to a 'No Parking' turning point. This allows walkers to disembark.

Go back down to the pond and turn left towards White Moss. About three-quarters of a mile south of the village of Rydal is Scandale Bridge, spanning Scandale Beck. Just before the bridge, and at the left of the road there are two separate places where you can park. The walk finishes at the gates of a meadow road that has a small lodge at its end. This is the picking-up point.

The Walk

1. Walk forward along the road. On your left there is a small pool rich in plant and insect life. You may be lucky in seeing the heron that lives among the tall reeds.

2. Just past the last cottage the metalled road becomes a track. This descends slightly as it rounds the fellside towards Brockstone House.

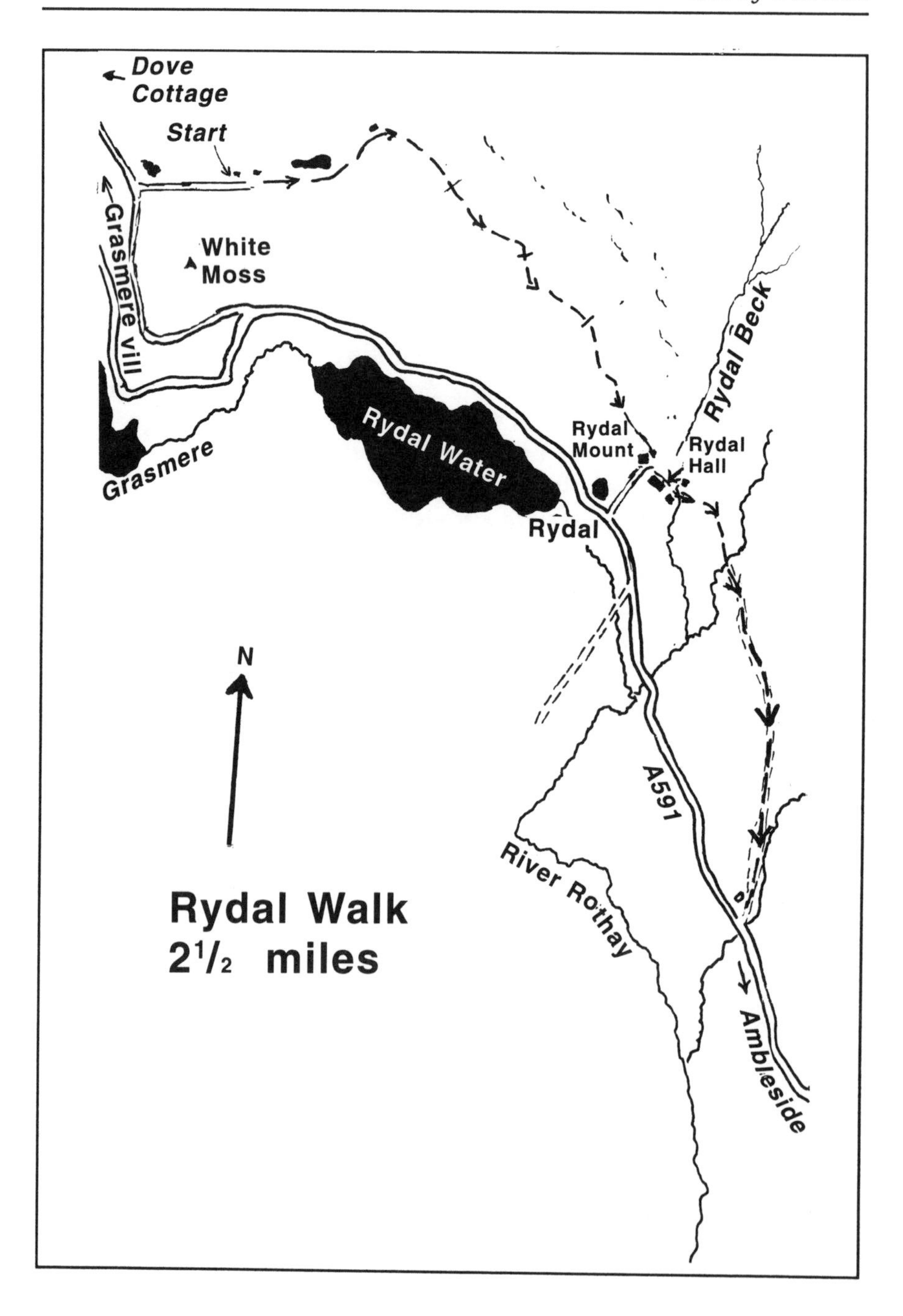
Dove Cottage
Start
White Moss
Grasmere vill
Grasmere
Rydal Water
Rydal Beck
Rydal Mount
Rydal Hall
Rydal
N
A591
River Rothay
Ambleside
Rydal Walk
2½ miles

3. having served its purpose for the house, the track becomes a path and its way is through a wicket gate.

4. The path continues through several gates along the lower slopes of Nab Scar. Below can be seen fleeting vehicles on the busy A591. That does not detract, however, from the peaceful rural scene.

5. Passing from the last field, continue along a walled track until you reach a minor road. Turn down it. On your right you will see Rydal Mount, the home for over 30 years, until his death, of William Wordsworth.

6. To the left is the entrance to Rydal Hall. Look for the finger post directing you to Ambleside. Turn as directed by the sign, and go forward around the side of the hall.

The Hall is now a residential centre and there are many signs of activity around the buildings. To interest the walker there is a small tearoom to the left.

8. The path crosses two becks. The first, however, Rydal Beck, cannot be ignored as it tumbles on its way past the buildings.

9. Soon it becomes an easy and pleasant walk. Rydal Park, the last part of the walk, invites you to tarry, given good weather. Just ahead of you, at the gates of the park, is the picking-up point.

24. Side Pike to Dungeon Ghyll

Length of walk: $1^1/_2$ miles

Map ref: NY 291051 (Outdoor Leisure Map No 6)

Starting height: 735ft (224 m)

Finishing height: 280ft (85.2 m)

Walk the lower slopes of a lesser fell, Side Pike, and there is the excitement of being among some of the giants. The imposing names are there. To the west lie Crinkle Crags, Bow Fell, Esk Pike and ahead the Langdale Pikes. Many well-known tracks can be seen – striking up The Band – (a spontaneous and unregretted pun), zig-zagging up Rossett Gill and treading a newly-laid way by Stickle Gill.

Driver

The dropping-off point is reached by going along the Langdale Valley on the B5343. After passing Wall End Farm the road rises and you need to negotiate some tight bends. A cattle grid is reached. This is the dropping-off point.

Turn in the road, and head back until you reach the car park opposite the side road leading to the Dungeon Ghyll Hotel. The car park is your picking-up point.

The Walk

1. Near the cattle grid is a stile. Climb over the wall then turn left.

2. Walk down the side of the wall by a well-defined path. The way is rather steep.

The delightful scenery should tempt you to dawdle awhile particularly if you have camera or binoculars.

3. Turn right as you near the trees and walk along by the wire fence.

4. There is a well-trodden path that takes you above the camp site.

5. The Langdale Pikes are to your left and there is an excellent view of the Crinkles behind you. You are walking on the slopes of Side Pike.

6. Pass through a gate and go straight ahead. The path is slightly less distinct and boggy.

7. You join a path coming in from the left. Walk straight on through a broken-down wall.

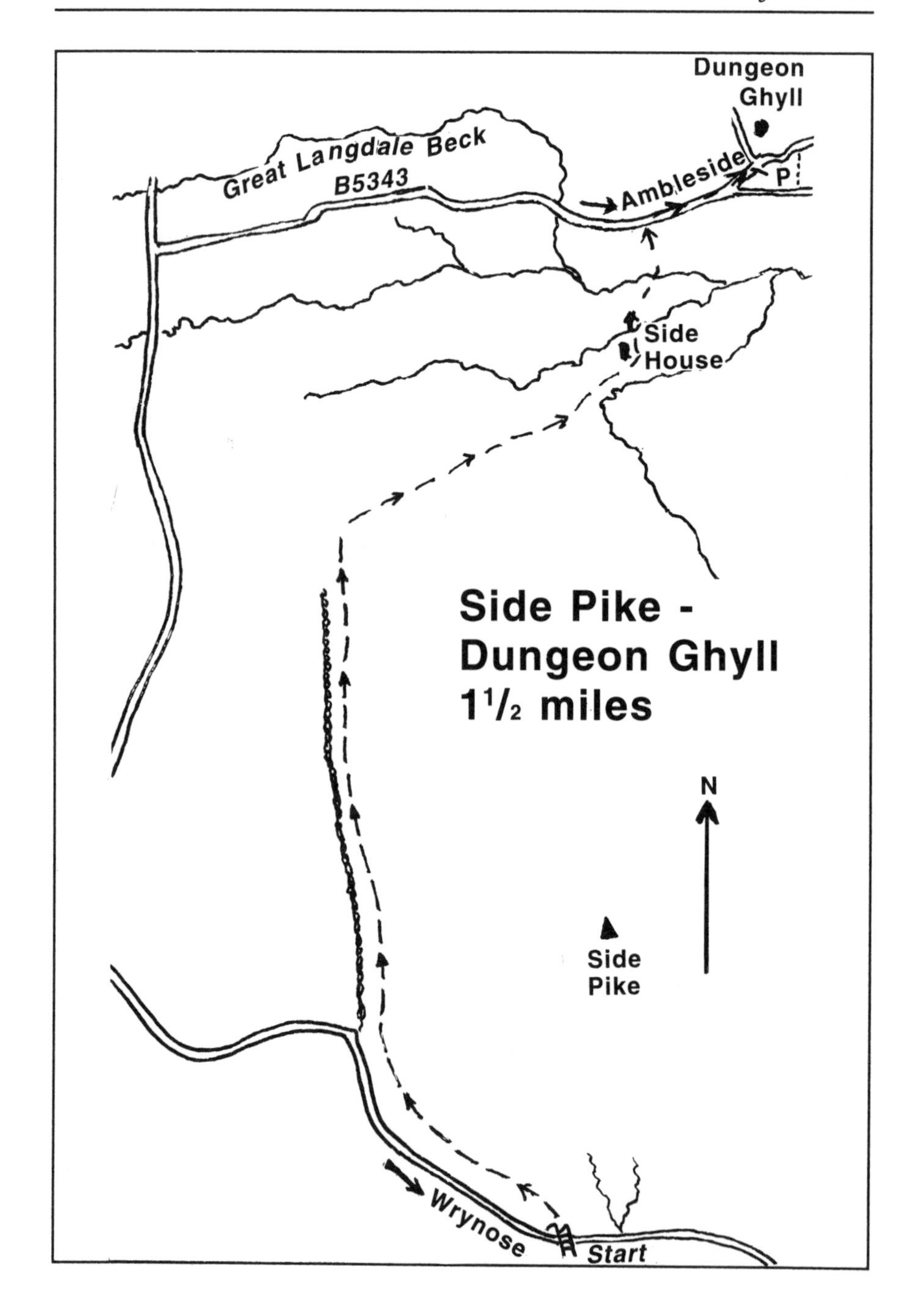
Dungeon
Ghyll
Great Langdale Beck
B5343
Ambleside
P
Side
House
Side Pike -
Dungeon Ghyll
1½ miles
N
Side
Pike
Wrynose
Start

8. Cross a small wooden foot bridge. Then, climb a wall stile. From here you can see Side House Farm which is reached by following a grassy path.

9. Turn through the farm yard and down the farm road to the B5343. Turn right and walk until you reach the car park on the right – your picking-up point.

25. Stock Ghyll

Length of walk: $2^3/_4$ miles

Map ref: NY 398077 (Outdoor Leisure Map No 7)

Starting height: 1150ft (350 m)

Finishing height: 400ft (122 m)

Although ending in Ambleside and on a well worn path amid fields the area in which the walk begins is in true upper fell land. In the first part of the walk there may be the sensation of going down the side of a large bowl. There is some protection from any wind until the path strikes south west. On the sky line there is much to view – the tops of fells lying on either side of Great

Langdale, and those beyond Grasmere. Views to the west of Loughrigg Fell may invite you to reflect that your walk started at a higher elevation than the summit of this lovely fell of many peaks. Find time to visit the waterfalls at Stock Ghyll. Their total drop is sixty feet. A compensation for any bad weather encountered is that cascades are then usually at their best.

Driver

The dropping-off point is near to the Kirkstone Pass Inn on the A592. You must take the Ambleside leg of the pass from its summit. After about 500 yards there is a parking area for about 8 cars on the left side of the road.

As the walk finishes in Ambleside, it is difficult to suggest a particular place as a picking-up point. It is perhaps best to point out that -

1. There is free parking outside the post office – very near to where the walk finishes,

2. There is parking in Kelsick Road,

3. There is a large car park at the northern end of Ambleside near to where Kirkstone Pass Road meets the A591.

The Walk

1. From the dropping-off point walk down the road until you see on the left a ruined structure, perhaps an animal shelter. You will see a finger post pointing the direction of the walk.

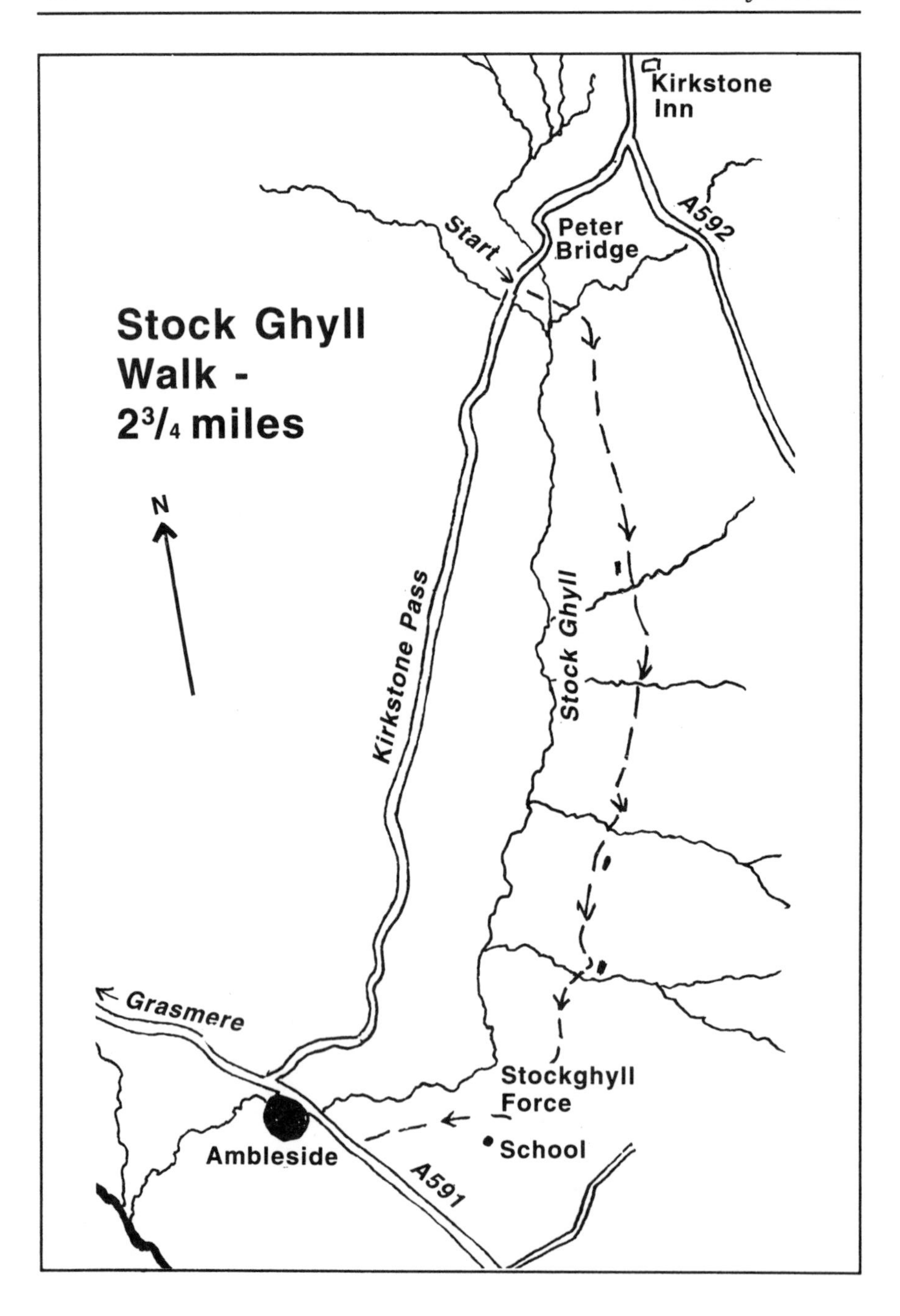

Kirkstone Inn
A592
Start
Peter Bridge
Stock Ghyll Walk - 2¾ miles
N
Kirkstone Pass
Stock Ghyll
Grasmere
Stockghyll Force
School
Ambleside
A591

2. The path is clearly defined starting between broken down walls then on a slightly downward way to the ghyll, with a view of Wansfell pike straight ahead.

3. There is a slight rise in the walk then a flattening-out as the path bends and follows the contours of the fell.

4. Near the 1,000 feet mark the first of the Groves, High Grove, is passed. It is a ruin and quite unlike its two mates further down the walk.

5. Views westwards compensate for the loss of path, replaced by a tarmacadam substitute. There are occasional peeps of the lake ahead.

6. The further groups of buildings – Middle and Low Grove – are passed, each well maintained and occupied.

7. Look for the way, and detour, to Stockghyll Force – it is signposted.

8. At a busier part of the walk you regain the main path. From there, you can walk straight down into town.

26. Steel End

Length of walk: 2 miles

Map ref: NY 327118 (Outdoor Leisure Map No 4)

Starting height: 745ft (230 m)

Finishing height: 620ft (189 m)

The whole area is fairly wild and desolate – ideal for urban escapism. The tramping of animals around the top of the farmland suggests grape-treading – without the grapes. The land around Wyth Burn seems forever wet, and defies its being used to much purpose. Sure footedness is required, as land barely two or three inches above lake level can be sodden. However, damp walking is soft walking, and easy on the joints.

It is to our advantage that the Water Board has opened up the lake-side to visitors. Now we can get close to Thirlmere and acquaint ourselves with water-level views.

Driver

The dropping point is on the A591 at the top of Dunmail Raise. Stop near the northern end of the dual carriageway. The grassy verge is wide enough to ensure safe disembarking.

To reach the picking-up point, go down the road towards Thirlmere. Near the bottom of the hill turn left and pass the entrance to Steel End Farm. Go round the western side of the lake and travel on for three-quarters of a mile and park in Dobgill car park, your meeting point.

The Walk

1. Walk on the grass verge down towards the lake.

2. There is a finger post to direct you on to the path. Go through the gate and head down towards the farm on the very narrow path.

3. It starts to leave the road side. Walk down by the wall on your right.

4. As you approach the farm the path gets a little rougher. Do not go to the far buildings but turn away from them towards a gate and stile.

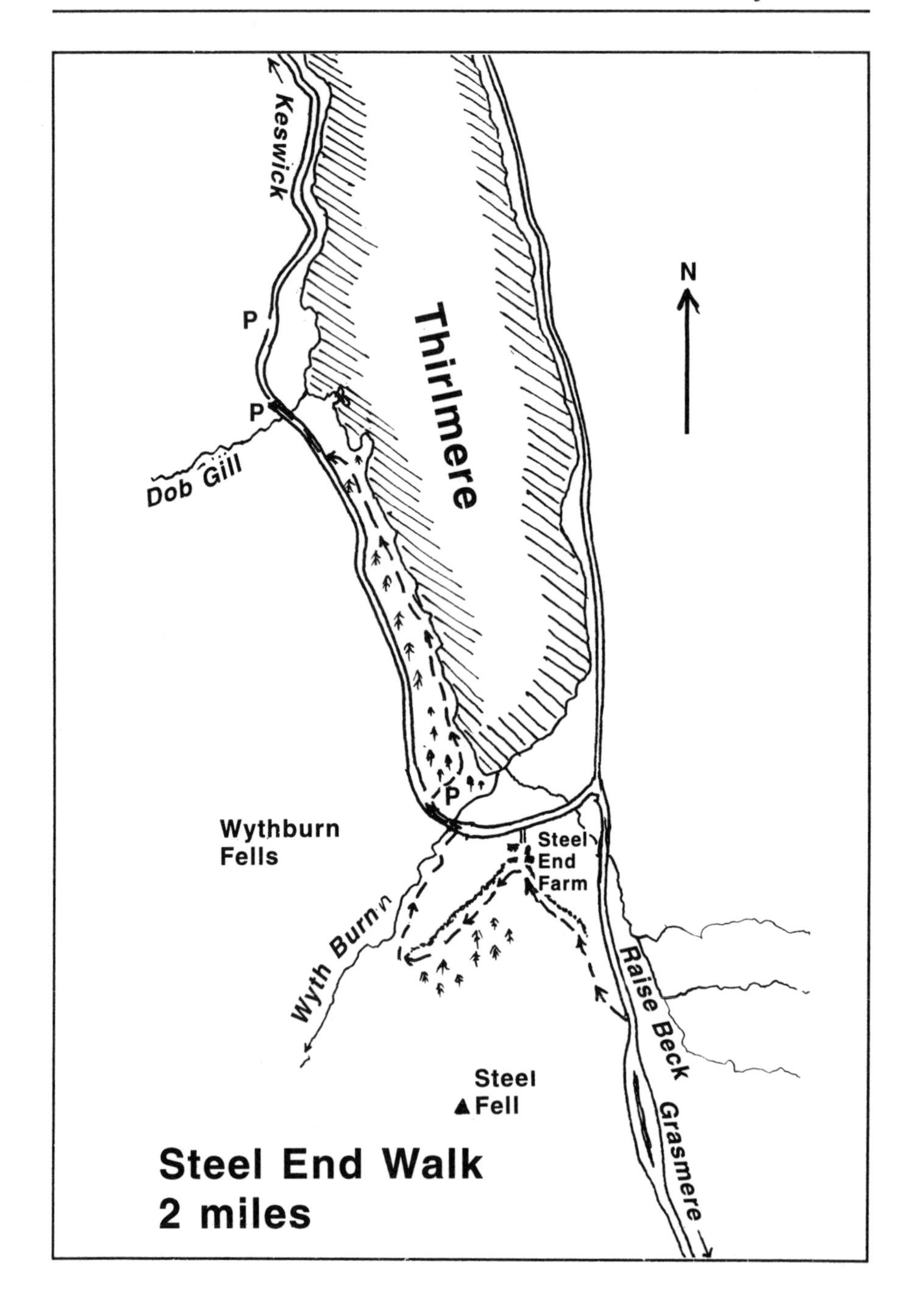
Keswick
P
P
Dob Gill
Thirlmere
N
P
Wythburn
Fells
Steel
End
Farm
Wyth Burn
Raise Beck
Grasmere
Steel
Fell
Steel End Walk
2 miles

5. The path rises slightly but just as soon heads downwards again. At the end of the wall there is a ladder stile. Go over it and walk down to the beck side. You need to pick your way carefully at times through and over wet rocks.

6. Ahead you will see the beck going under the road. You go along its side until you climb some rough steps up to a gate leading to the road.

7. Turn left and walk for 30 yards before turning right into a car park. This is not your picking-up point. Go forward through the gate at the other end.

8. Turn left along the path towards the lake. It can be quite damp at certain parts of the year.

9. Continue along the lakeside. The walk is flat but rough underfoot.

10. There are several obstructions – broken-down walls, fences, streams – to negotiate until the path turns to the left.

11. You will see a gap in the wall. You will need to take care as there is no pavement. Turn right and walk for about 50 yards to a car park on the left. This is the picking-up point.

27. Watendlath Beck

Length of walk: $1^{3}/_{4}$ miles

Map ref: NY 276164 (Outdoor Leisure Map No 4)

Starting height: 820ft (250 m)

Finishing height: 330ft (101 m)

The hamlet, made famous by Hugh Walpole, is well worth a browse. The bridge you must then cross is much photographed and features in many paintings of the district. The first half of the walk, as far as the wooden footbridge, has, in recent years, become well-trodden. People venture so far, then return to the car. It is the stretch that follows the beck that is much more private and peaceful. Through the trees there are glimpses of the valley below and the fells opposite.

On gaining the road, look back and upwards from whence you have come. You might want to do it all over again.

Driver

Leave Keswick by B5289, the Borrowdale Road. After 2 miles take the left fork, signposted 'Watendlath'. You need to travel for $2^3/_4$ miles before reaching the hamlet. It is a single track road with passing places. In summer it can be quite busy. At Watendlath there is a car park, the dropping point.

Retrace your steps to the main road. Turn left, a very sharp turn, and travel for about $1^1/_2$ miles to the Borrowdale Hotel, your picking-up point.

The Walk

1. Leave Watendlath by crossing the bridge. Go through the gate to the right and follow a well marked path. Walk along the side of the beck and up a slight rise to a stile in the wall.

2. The path is easy to follow between the fell side and the beck. Pause to look back at the view of the central fells.

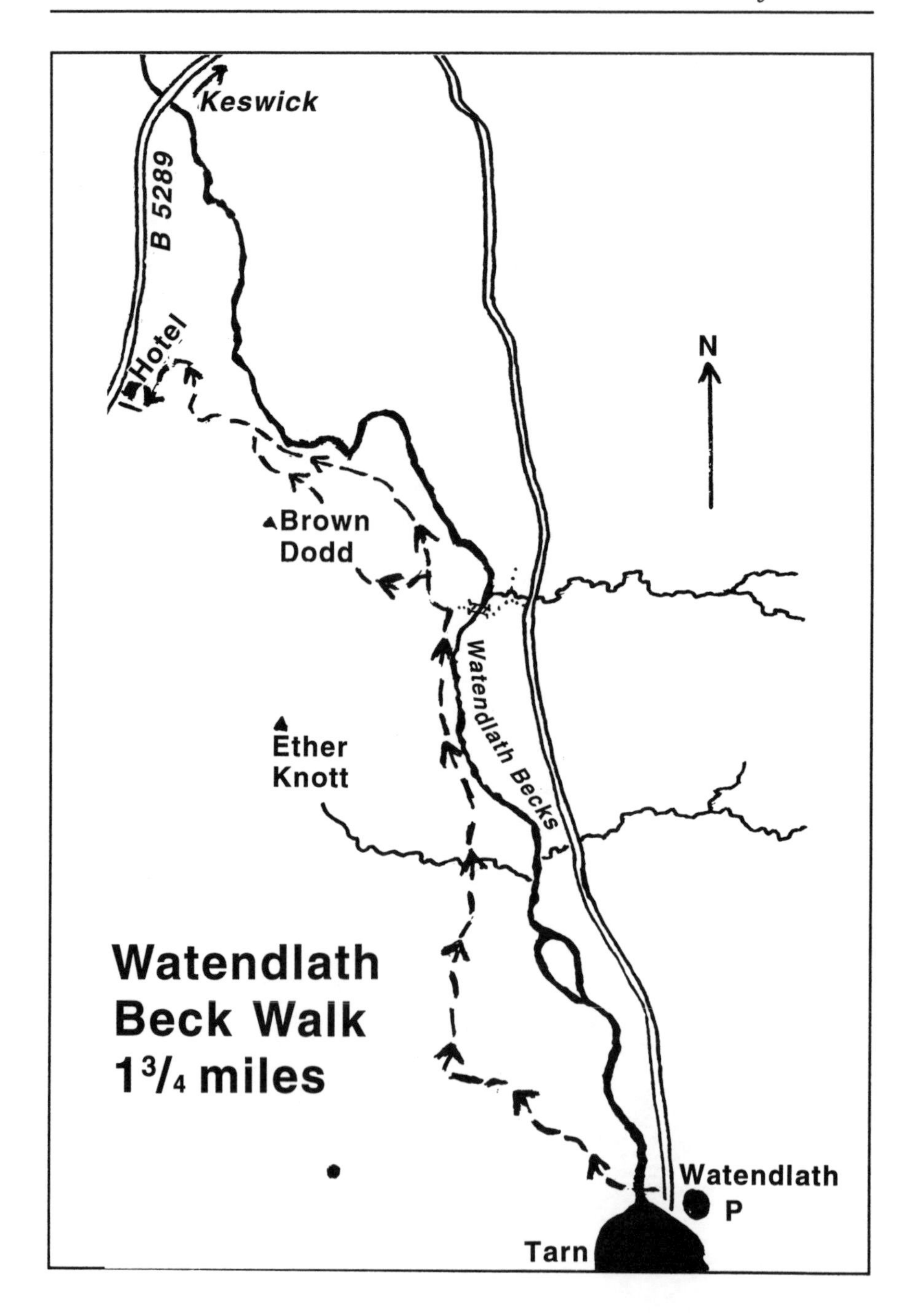
Keswick
B 5289
Hotel
N
Brown Dodd
Watendlath Becks
Ether Knott
Watendlath Beck Walk 1¾ miles
Watendlath
P
Tarn

3. The path has risen slightly. To redress, steps, both natural and man made, are descended and beck level is reached again.

4. The walk continues through a wooded beck side until a wooden bridge is sighted. Look for the direction sign set in the ground just before it. Leaving the beck, take the path that goes to Lodore.

5. Through the stile, the path takes you into woodland, Mossmire Coppice. The path is distinct but rather rough and wet.

6. The path descends, and, over a stile you see the beck again.

7. Turn left by the fence and walk across rough ground to another stile situated between the beck and the end of a wall.

8. Just where the path leaves the beck again, there is a very pleasant view of Derwentwater and Skiddaw beyond.

9. Continue until you reach a grassy Hause. If you have time, pause to scan the Borrowdale Valley below. Follow the pleasant but steep, grassy path down to the end of the walk.

28. Thornthwaite Forest

Length of walk: 2 miles

Map ref: NY 208245 (Outdoor Leisure Map No 4)

Starting height: 1075ft (327.5 m)

Finishing height: 300ft (91.5 m)

With recent additions and alterations at the Forest Centre this walk now has facilities for refreshments at each end. Despite the number of visitors, walking in the forest can be quiet and peaceful. Occasionally, people, young, old or middling, singly or in groups, appear from this path or that, all moving with intent. They may be holding Forest Maps, or Orienteering Maps.

Walkers, and participants in "the thinking sport" are welcome in this forest.

From vantage points on the walk there is much to be seen, in the Vale of Keswick and away to the east. Across from the foot of Bassenthwaite is the other part of Thornthwaite Forest, planted on and around Dodd. One last sight to look for is The Bishop, – a prominent, white rock, the profile of which suggests the head of a bishop, complete with mitre. It protrudes from the side of Barf. A yard of ale is the reward for anyone who can scale, then paint it. New Year's Eve is a favourite time for attempts!

Driver

The setting-down point is in the parking area at the Visitors' Centre of Thornthwaite Forest. This is reached by leaving the A591, driving through the village of Braithwaite on the B5292 then through the Whinlatter Pass for two miles until the Centre is reached.

The pick up point is reached by going back down to Braithwaite. Just after passing the Royal Oak Hotel on the right, turn to the left past the village school. Continue on the minor side road for 2 miles through the village of Thornthwaite and on to the Swan Hotel. There is a small parking area opposite the hotel at the end of the walk. If you intend to visit the hotel, then parking space is at its door.

The Walk

This is one of those ideal walks where all mod cons are provided. At the Visitors' Centre there is shelter and toilets and at the end of the walk, if well-timed, refreshments at the Swan Hotel.

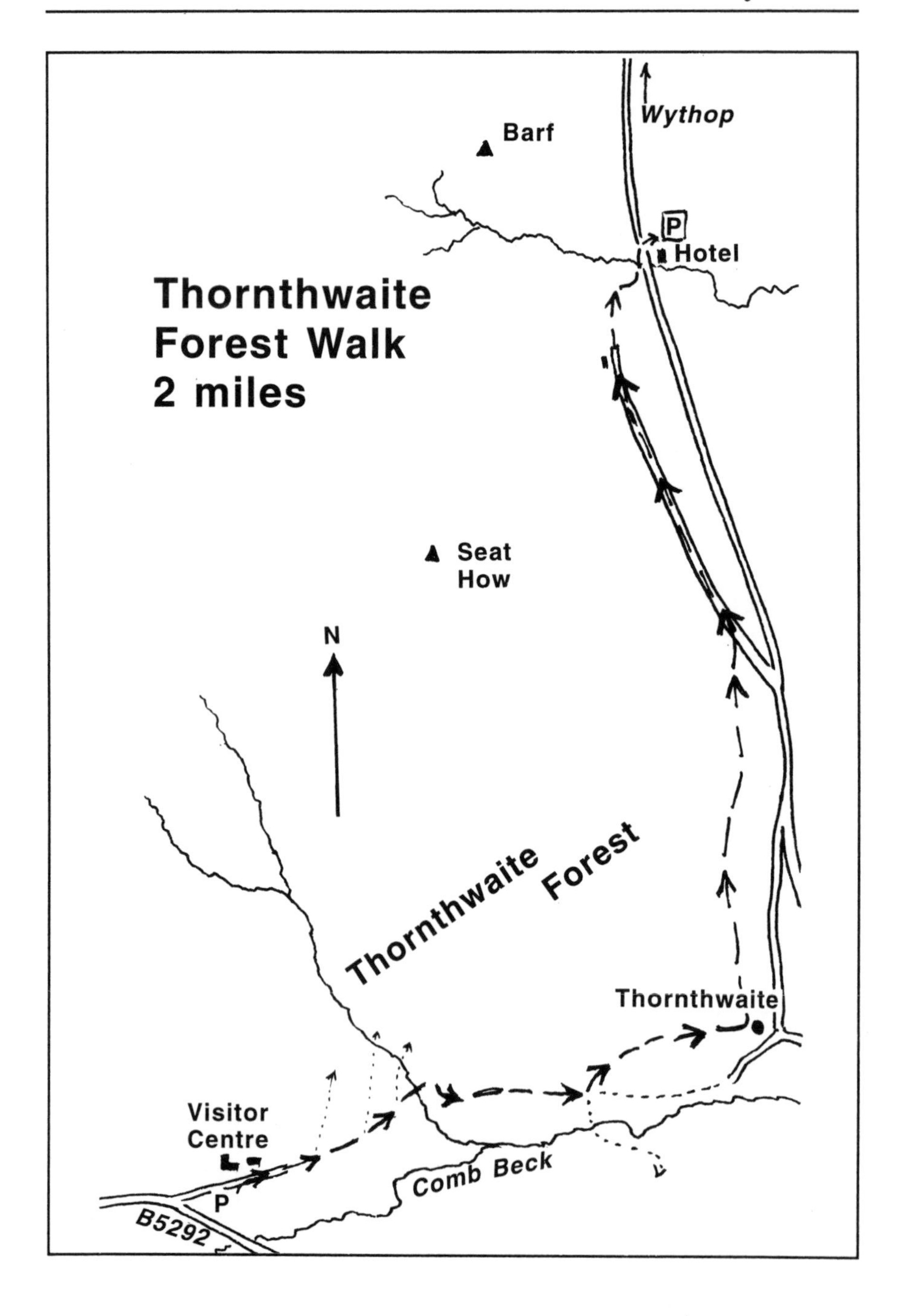
Wythop
Barf
P
Hotel
Thornthwaite
Forest Walk
2 miles
Seat
How
N
Thornthwaite Forest
Thornthwaite
Visitor
Centre
P
Comb Beck
B5292

1. From the car park take the forest road immediately below the Visitors' Centre. Ignore the road leading up and to the left and walk past a bungalow on the right.

2. At the next fork take the road to the right. As the land continues to drop, pass by a road going off to the right.

3. From that fork, and about 40 yards ahead, can be seen two very tall conifers on the side edge of the forest road. Midway between the two trees you will find a narrow path leading straight down the fell side. That is your way.

4. This is a particularly fine forest path that leads to a glade in which a beck has to be crossed. Ignore a small path leading off to the right.

5. Continue down the path until a forest road is reached. Turn left on to the road and continue on it around the side of the fell. There are fine views immediately below you, across the Vale of Keswick and beyond.

6. The forest road ends at a triangular gate. Do not use the stile – it is unsafe and very slippery when wet.

7. When you reach the farm road a few yards on, turn left and follow it. It is a good terrace walk taking you past Barf Cottage and so to a crossing of Beckstones Gill. Across the ford a right-hand turn in the road brings you to the picking-up point opposite the Swan Hotel.

29. Stone Circle to Rough How

Length of walk: $2^3/_4$ miles

Map ref: NY 292237 (Outdoor Leisure Map No 4)

Starting height: 680ft (207.2 m)

Finishing height: 510ft (155.5 m)

The Stone Circle attracts lots of visitors, many of whom park, walk to the Circle, then drive off again. This walk extends the visit. There are three parts to it. The first is a field walk, the second, a meadow walk. In season, fully grown grasses and wild flowers are a superb sight. The third part of the walk is along a quiet, narrow farm road, with interesting buildings, some of which are modern, added to old, with no jarring. This road leads on to a bridle path under the shelter of the western side of High Rigg – more popularly known as Naddle Fell.

Driver

Leave Keswick by A5271. At a junction with the Windermere Road go left, as though to Penrith, but turn right immediately up a minor road sign posted 'Stone Circle'. The dropping point is two-thirds of a mile up this road by the Stone Circle.

If coming from the south on the A591, pass its junction with B5322 and go on for just over 3 miles. At the crest of the hill a narrow road joins from the right – Castle Lane. Travel along this to its end, the dropping-off point.

To reach the picking-up point you need to go back to the Windermere Road, the A591. This can be gained by going along Castle Lane or by going back down the minor road towards Keswick then turning left at the main road junction, on to the A591 to Windermere. Travel back down the road for just over $1^1/_2$ miles. Look out for a stretch of old road, now signed as a parking area, on your left. This is the picking-up point.

The Walk

1. After being dropped at the Stone Circle, time could be spent at the monument. Then, from the parking area, go towards Goosewell Farm, slightly downhill, to a finger post on the right side of the road.

2. The path will take you between the Stone Circle site and a small tree plantation.

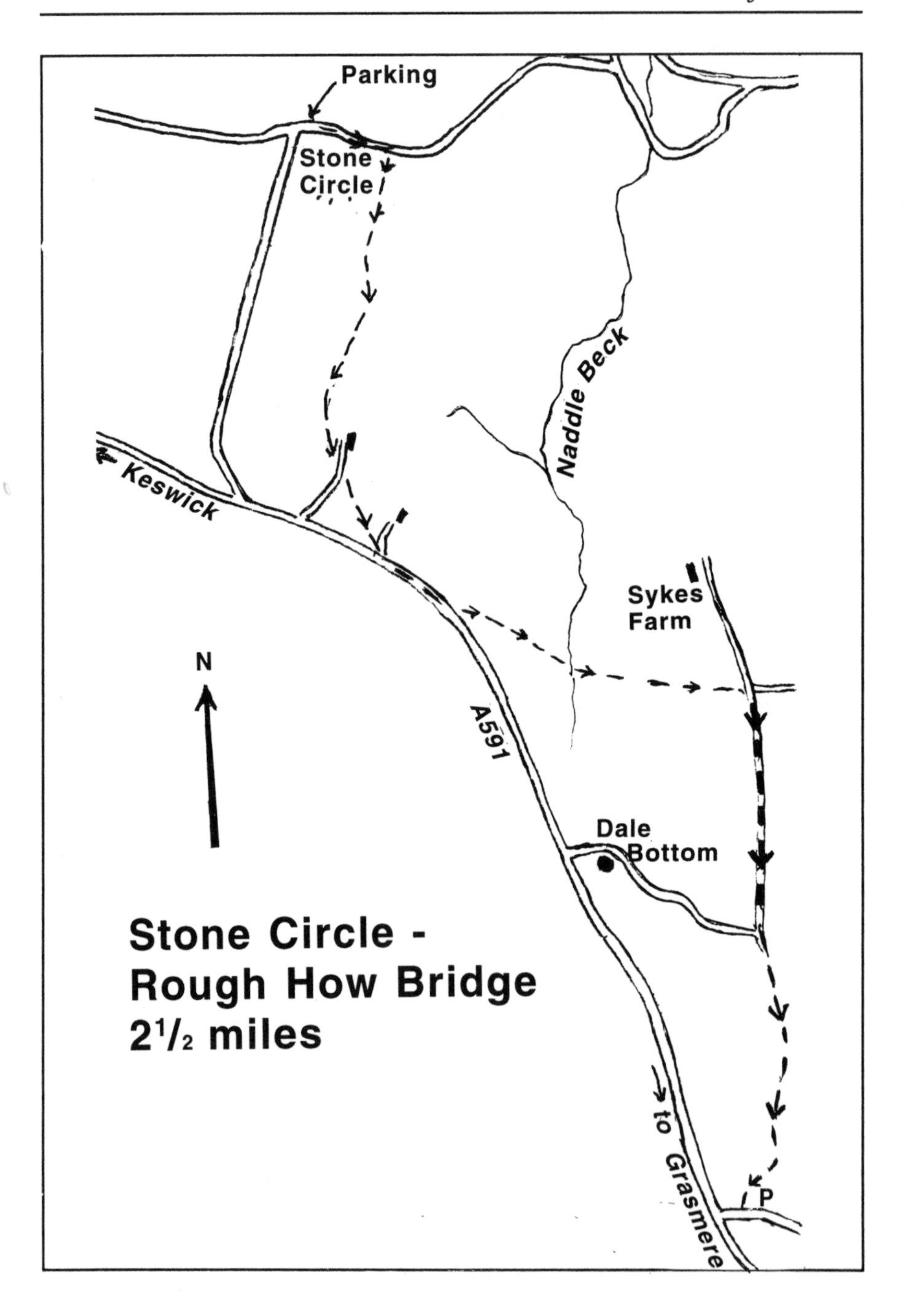
Parking
Stone Circle
Naddle Beck
Keswick
Sykes Farm
N
A591
Dale Bottom
Stone Circle - Rough How Bridge
2 1/2 miles
to Grasmere
P

3. Follow the well-defined path across three fields heading for a small copse. Walk the bridle path past picturesque High Nest until a gate is reached as the path turns towards the right.

4. Go through the gate and cross diagonally a damp, sloping field. The drive to Low Nest is gained and it is but a short walk to the A591.

5. 50 yards down the road from the drive there is a finger post directing you to St John's Church. Climb the wall stile and start diagonally across the field.

6. You come to another wall stile. Enter the field but take note of the farmer's request that you keep to its edge. Follow the wall around until you cross into the next field.

7. At a path junction a finger post instructs you to 'Turn left'. Continue along the path until a farm road is reached.

8. Sykes Farm is to the left, St John's Church straight ahead. You turn right and continue along the farm road. There is a road to the right but you continue straight ahead between walls.

9. Past the last house, the road becomes a path. There is a slight rise to a finger post and a split in the path – take the right leg.

10. A further rise in the path, which is following the side of a wall, leads you to a stile. Continue along the bridle path with its slight rise, then drop down to a gate.

11. Go through the gate, on to another, then to the last stile and to the parking area, your picking-up point.

30. Tilberthwaite

Length of walk: 2 miles

Map ref: NY 318033 (Outdoor Leisure Map No 7)

Starting height: 460ft (140.2 m)

Finishing height: 350ft (106.7 m)

Little Langdale, the setting for the start of this walk was carved out by ice flowing from the west, thus creating a hanging valley and tarn. Many see the tarn from a distance but few walk its shores, maybe because of the many beds of reeds around it denoting boggy land. This does not deter wild life of which there is plenty.

Slaters Bridge is an interesting construction, built by quarry men to enable them to get to work in a dry state.

Further along the river, but not to be crossed, is a rather ugly bridge and a ford. The river can be swift and deep at times here. Finally in the hamlet there is a farm building housing a photogenic Spinning Gallery.

Driver

Leave the A593 (Ambleside to Coniston) road and turn for Wrynose Pass. Just past Little Langdale Village there is a road junction with one coming in from the right from Elterwater. This is the dropping point.

To reach the picking-up point, retrace your journey to the A593. Turn right on it and travel for 3 miles in the direction of Coniston. Look for the very sharp turn to the right on a road signposted to Tilberthwaite. Travel for 1 mile to a large parking area near a bridge over a beck. This is the picking-up point.

The Walk

1. Take the Birk Howe Farm road. The sign at the beginning tells you that it is a public footpath.

2. As you get to the farm entrance a sign points you towards Slaters Bridge. With Little Langdale Tarn on your right, cross over three fields, and go down to the bridge.

3. Time should be spent at the bridge. Then cross over it and go forward to a wall-stile, by which you get on to a farm track.

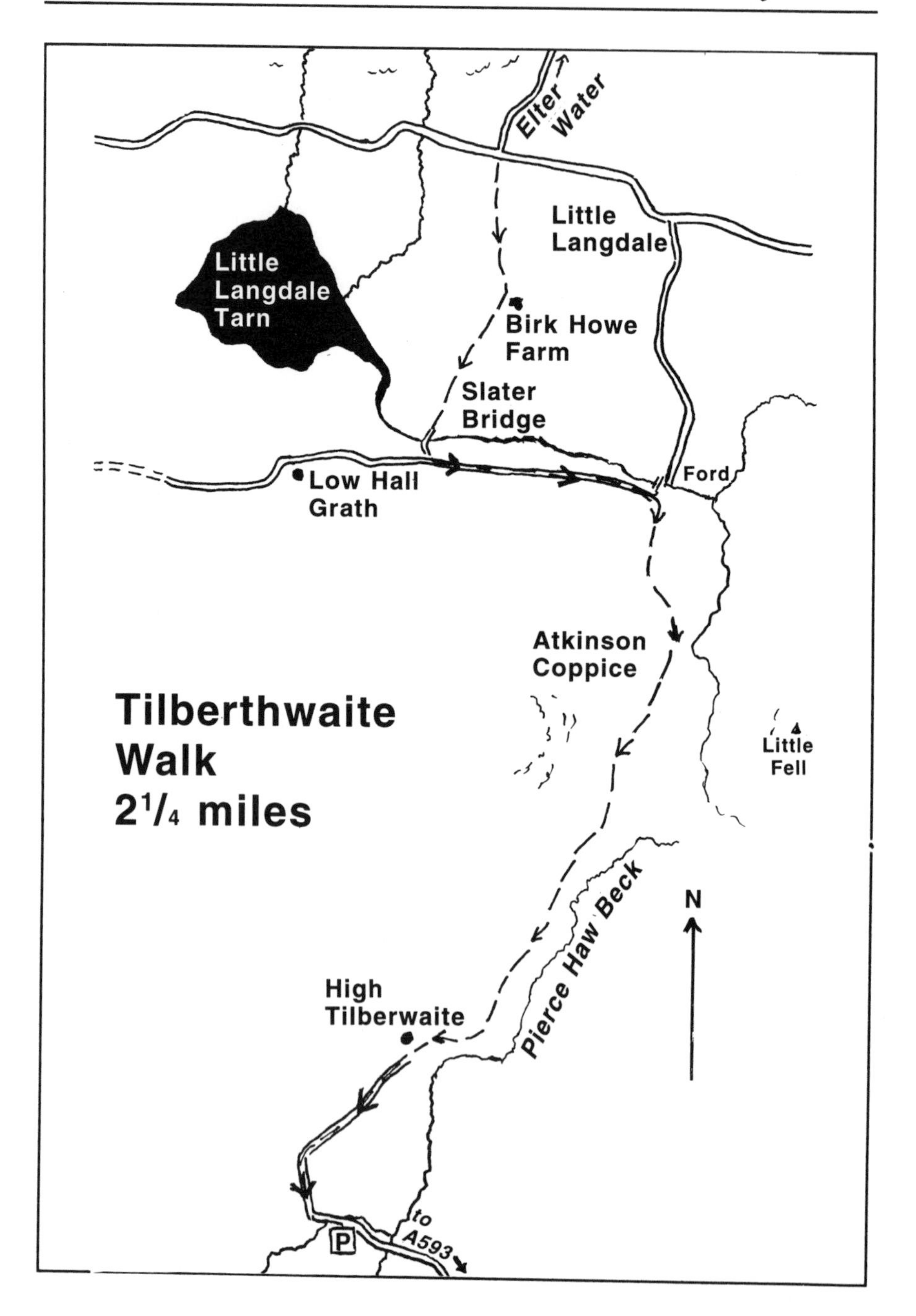
Elter Water
Little Langdale
Little Langdale Tarn
Birk Howe Farm
Slater Bridge
Low Hall Grath
Ford
Atkinson Coppice
Tilberthwaite Walk
2¼ miles
Little Fell
Pierce Haw Beck
N
High Tilberwaite
P
to A593

4. Turn left and go along the track until you reach a second bridge and a ford. Turn right, away from them.

5. As you enter the woodland take the right of the two paths before you.

6. There is a slight rise in the path as you pass a building on the right. The path goes through woodland, with that of the National Trust to your left.

7. There are paths joining you first from the left then the right. Press on with Pierce How Beck on your left.

8. There is a slight rise as you approach High Tilberthwaite Farm, then a drop as you reach a gate. Pass through on to a tarmacadam road.

9. From here to the picking-up point you walk the road. The hedges on the side are very rich and unspoilt. White painted houses are to your right, one of which has a spinning gallery.